Scholars &Rebels

in Nineteenth-Century Ireland

For Ricca Edmundson and Markus Wörner

Scholars &Rebels

in Nineteenth-Century Ireland

Terry Eagleton

BLACKWELL
Publishers

First published 1999

2 4 6 8 10 9 7 5 3 1

Blackwell Publishers Ltd
108 Cowley Road
Oxford OX4 1JF
UK

Blackwell Publishers Inc.
350 Main Street
Malden, Massachusetts 02148
USA

British Library Cataloguing in Publication Data

A CIP catalogue record for this book is available from the British Library.

Library of Congress Cataloging-in-Publication Data

Eagleton, Terry, 1943–
    Scholars and rebels in nineteenth-century Ireland / Terry
Eagleton.
        p.   cm.
    Includes bibliographical references and index.
    ISBN 0-631-21445-3 (hbk : alk. paper). — ISBN 0-631-21446-1
(pbk : alk. paper)
    1. Ireland—Intellectual life—19th century.   2. English
literature—Irish authors—History and criticism.   3. English
literature—19th century—History and criticism.   4. Politics and
literature—Ireland—History—19th century.   5. Dublin (Ireland)—
Intellectual life—19th century.   6. Revolutionaries—Ireland
Biography.   7. Scholars—Ireland Biography.   8. Irish language—
Revival.   I. Title.
DA950.1.E24 1999
306'.09418'35—dc21   99-34968
                                                                CIP

Typeset in 10½ on 13½ pt Meridien by Ace Filmsetting Ltd, Frome
Printed in Great Britain by TJ International, Padstow, Cornwall

This book is printed on acid-free paper

Contents

Preface

This book is the final volume in a trilogy of studies of Irish culture, of which the first two were *Heathcliff and the Great Hunger* (Verso, 1995) and *Crazy John and the Bishop* (Cork University Press, 1998). Like its predecessors, the present work concerns itself less with isolated authors than with cultural movements and conceptual currents. Like those books too, it tries to resist the rather canonical bent of Irish literary studies by retrieving some minor figures and salvaging some neglected reputations. It also tries to resist the rather narrow range of interests of much in that field. Its focus is on the extraordinary ferment of intellectual life in mid-nineteenth-century Dublin, all the way from politics to medicine, cultural history to political economy. In such a brief span, any such treatment has to be selective, and the book has its fair share of skimmings and exclusions. But I have tried to register something of the wealth of intellectual preoccupations of this remarkable community, and to frame it theoretically with some reflections on the nature of intellectual work in general and its place in political life.

T.E.
Dublin, 1999

1

Colonial Intellectuals

Not all intellectuals are intelligent, and not all the intelligent are intellectuals. The word 'intellectual', like 'hairdresser' or 'chief executive', denotes a social function rather than a personal quality. It is this which is misunderstood by those who, despising intellectuals as effete or subversive, feel compelled to add a 'so-called' or '*soi-disant*' to the term, for fear of paying an unintended compliment to those they are out to lampoon. Though they disapprove of intellectuals as such, they still feel the need to acquit themselves of philistinism by suggesting that the particular set of intellectuals under fire are a fraudulent variety of the breed. One may thus dismiss intellectuals as such while speciously retrieving one's respect for real intelligence.

If intellectuals pose a problem for modern-day philistines, they represented a rather more complex kind of dilemma for the Victorians, who both feared and admired knowledge. Knowledge was what drove the great march of progress forward, as traditional learning shattered into a hundred different specialisms, and a new breed of technical intellectuals sprang up (scientists, bureaucrats, engineers, administrators and the like) who harnessed this learning to the business of developing industrial production. But the same knowledge, with its secularizing, disenchanting bent, also threatened to undermine a good many traditional pieties and sanctions; and it was these which lent stability to the very social order in which progress was running its course. Since these values involved custom, reverence, tradition, intuition, they were in danger of being rationalized out of existence by a more pragmatic, professional kind of intelligence. It is an ambivalence which runs through the work of Alfred Tennyson, for whom 'knowledge' and 'wisdom', an enthusiasm for technological progress and a wariness of its hubris, are increasingly at loggerheads. From Coleridge to Ruskin, the Victorian sage thus becomes a type of Antonio Gramsci's 'traditional' intellectual, fostering an anti-modern faith in transcendent value and disinterested inquiry, while the scientists, political agitators and social engineers play the part of Gramsci's 'organic' intelligentsia, as social functionaries for whom knowledge has a practical, emancipatory force.[1] We shall see how this new version of the quarrel between ancients and moderns affects nineteenth-century Irish society too. When the lawyer Isaac Butt speaks of true 'mental culture' as at war with 'the scepticism and materialism of the age', he speaks as a traditional intellectual.[2]

But the opposition between 'traditional' and 'organic' is notably unstable. The historian W. E. H. Lecky distinguishes two 'great classes of writers': those who 'represent faithfully and express strongly the dominant tendencies, opinions, habits, characteristics of their age, collecting as in a focus the half-formed thoughts that are prevailing around them, giving them an articulate voice, and by the force of their advocacy greatly strengthening them', and those more original writers who stand askew to the conventional wisdom of their time.[3] Lecky's first category – 'echoes', as he somewhat disparagingly calls them – resemble Gramsci's organic intellectuals in their role as organizers and articulators of popular current of ideas, but differ from them in their consolidatory rather than critical function. Lecky clearly has in mind here popularizers, journalistic hacks and the more commercially minded men of letters, for none of whom he has much time. His second category – 'voices', as he calls them – are sages or traditional intellectuals in their aloofness from this public arena, but exactly because of this distance fulfil something of the critical function assigned by Gramsci to the organic intelligentsia. It is because Gramsci's organic intellectuals are for the most part the representatives of an *oppositional* group or class that they can be both critics and articulators of popular opinion, roles which for the patrician Lecky are necessarily at odds.

In one sensW˙ intellectuals can be defined as the opposite of academics. Broadly speaking, academics are obviously to be ranked among the intellectuals, given that they professionally trade in ideas. In a more exact sense of the term, however, most academics are by no means intellectuals. For one thing, the classical intellectual tends to move between different subject-areas, whereas the academic is typically confined to a single specialism. And if intellectuals feel the need for this mobility of mind, it is because they are concerned with the bearing of ideas on society as a whole, which is hardly the case with the majority of those who populate the universities.[4] Jean-Paul Sartre deemed a nuclear scientist to be an intellectual only if he had signed a petition against nuclear testing. Intellectuals occupy a public sphere, while academics, even if they are state-funded, conduct a more private sort of existence. Nineteenth-century Ireland's premier scholarly institution, Trinity College Dublin, passed from being an intellectual centre in mid-century, when men like Isaac Butt and Thomas Davis used national sentiment to bridge the gap between ideas and political life, to becoming something of an academic enclave by the end of the century. Scholars like Edward Dowden[5] retreat to a more cloistered intellectual style, in the teeth of a Gaelic nationalism which helped to maroon them from the public sphere. The movement is mirrored in the career from mid-century to *fin-de-siècle* of the historian W. E. H. Lecky, youthful liberal nationalist turned crusty conservative scholar.

At different times and in different places, one or more of the discourses of academia find themselves providing a temporary home for what might more properly be called intellectual activity. The locus of intellectual life thus tends to revolve, as this or that academic discipline is selected as its hub as the historical situation requires. Given its rather blurred definition, 'English' has played this role for a century and a half in Britain, just as philosophy has long fulfilled the function in parts of modern Europe, and theology had performed it earlier. Among other things, it is the fact that

English studies are of embarrassingly low definition which has allowed them to play host to a motley crew of concerns, many of
which are only loosely literary. This was as true of Coleridge as it is
of Cultural Studies. A subject which seems to deal with everything
from death to dactyls, similes to sexuality, ethics to epigrams, will
tend to attract intellectuals (or 'theorists' as they are called today)
alongside academics, not least because the stuff of literature – language – is also the medium of culture as a whole, the pivot between
text and society.

This is not an especially welcome development, since those reared
in the disciplines of literary criticism are not usually adept at what is
normally called thinking. The phrase 'literary theory', like the phrase
'military intelligence', thus has an unavoidably oxymoronic ring to
it. Literary critics trade in sensuous particulars, shifts of tone, turns
of syntax, much more than they do in systematic ideas – so that the
fact that it is they, of all people, who have come in our time increasingly to take on 'intellectual' functions is perhaps already the sign
of a certain crisis. One can only be grateful that it is areas like epistemology and psychoanalysis they have muscled in on, rather than
surgery or aeronautical engineering. If they have done so, however,
it has been a matter of historical necessity as much as intellectual
hubris. It is the *trahison* of the *clercs* surrounding them which has led
among other things to the mildly farcical spectacle of those trained
to spot a metonymy making solemn pronouncements on the nature
of the human subject, or those skilled in noting a prolepsis holding
forth on the uncertain nature of knowledge. Once sociology falls
prey to positivism, philosophy to linguistic analysis and psychology
to behaviourism, they are likely to jettison as so much surplus
conceptual baggage a number of large ethical, political and metaphysical questions to which people still clamour for answers; and it
has been the unenviable destiny of literary or cultural studies in our
time to be on hand to scoop them up.

The word 'intellectual' as a noun dates from the nineteenth century, with some isolated, sometimes pejorative, earlier uses. The
word first enters English dictionaries in the 1880s as an adjective
rather than a noun, to denote a capacity for superior forms of
knowledge; at the very close of the century, via the Dreyfusards, it

gathers a collective political connotation. T. W. Heyck argues that Victorian England had three categories of intellectuals – scientists, scholars and men of letters – but no meta-category to cover them all.[6] In the twentieth century, a new but related term, 'intelligentsia', is borrowed from the Russian, to denote self-conscious groups of politically oppositional thinkers.[7] Whereas intellectuals may be private, isolated figures, an intelligentsia shows some awareness of itself as a social caste, one bred by a modernizing state yet often enough, not least in colonial conditions, alienated from that state by over-education, baulked social ambitions and a history of political oppression.[8] This is true enough of nineteenth-century Ireland, where banking and commerce remained largely in Protestant hands, and where there was an overproduction of poorly salaried school-teachers. The colonial state, with its administrative and educational requirements, brings into existence a new breed of clerkly technocrats, educated professionals caught in a bind between their metropolitan aspirations and their native lack of advancement. They thus become one fertile source of political nationalism.

The modernizing, integrating thrust of the British state in nineteenth-century Ireland, from the reorganizing of the Board of Works to the Poor Law, the police force, the Ordnance Survey, the national schools and the opening of civil service admission to competitive examination, brought in its wake a burgeoning bureaucracy, a massive expansion of the civil service and hence a spectacular increase in (in the broad, Gramscian sense of the term) the intelligentsia. Civil service recruitment increased ten-fold from 1861 to 1911, with Catholics leaping dramatically from 39 to 61 per cent of the staff as educational reform earlier in the century bore its belated fruit.[9] The end of the nineteenth century thus sees an upsurge of a Catholic intelligentsia, just as the political decline of the Ascendancy is spurring it into renewed cultural life. It was the fusion of these two groups which became known as the Literary Revival, as two dying cultures came uneasily together. An Anglo-Irish gentry on the wane sought to refurbish itself by gingerly linking arms with a nationalist Catholic middle class, while the intellectual leaders of that class were busy fashioning an identity for themselves from the even more moribund civilization of ancient Gaelic Ireland.

The intelligentsia, then, are in part functionaries of the state, whereas the intellectuals move largely within civil society. In this sense, patriotic eighteenth-century Irish scholars like Charles O'Conor or Sylvester O'Halloran might best be seen as 'intellectuals', whereas nationalist activists like Patrick Pearse, D. P. Moran and Arthur Griffith belong to a more modern 'intelligentsia'. The Young Irelanders also stemmed for the most part from an urban, professional, legal or journalistic background, in contrast to the profiles of more traditional Irish intellectuals such as Lecky or William Rowan Hamilton. The social *ressentiment* thesis about nationalism applies fairly well to internal exiles like Pearse, Moran and Griffith, along with Fintan Lalor and a handful of other Young Irelanders; but it hardly accounts for the national sentiments of such Anglo-Irish luminaries as William Stokes, William Wilde and the younger W. E. H. Lecky, who as the flower of the Dublin Ascendency establishment can scarcely be said to have felt socially excluded. These Ascendancy intellectuals, in their intimate face-to-face networks, formed a self-conscious intelligentsia; and if it was critical and mildly dissident, in the manner of intelligentsias, it is because its members felt sidelined rather than socially thwarted, as Anglo-Irishmen in a militantly Gaelic milieu. As 'traditional' intellectuals, in Gramsci's sense of the word,[10] they could seek a new role by placing their formidable intellectual resources at the service of the very national movement which was threatening to oust them. It is as though they could resolve their own particular crisis of identity only by throwing in their lot with the rather different identity crisis of the nation as a whole.

In doing this, they remain for the most part traditional intellectuals, upper-middle-class, often amateur scholars who find themselves more at home in academia and the gentleman's club than (like John Mitchel, Pearse, Griffith or Moran) in newspaper offices, the national schools or the civil service. But their political insecurity also compels them into forms of collaborative work and political intervention which are more usually associated with Gramsci's organic intelligentsia; and this, as we shall see, throws some light on the paradoxes of their remarkable organ, the *Dublin University Magazine* (*DUM*). Moreover, the main contribution which some of these

6

genteel scholars made to the national culture – the Ordnance Survey of 1824 to 1841 – drew them directly into the state apparatus, in the manner of a more administrative intelligentsia.[11] The Survey, the single most ambitious intellectual enterprise of nineteenth-century Ireland, was state-funded partly because no Irish institution could have afforded it; so that it was the weakness of Irish civil society which helped to produce a centralized state. William Wilde, in most ways a traditional intellectual, was to win his knighthood through his work on an equally 'modern' project, the national census. These men were a hybrid of the traditional and the modern intellectual; and much the same applies to those Gaelic nationalist intellectuals who, trained in modern vocations but denied preferment, fell back on a nativist, anti-modern ideology in order to achieve their eminently up-to-date ends. If nationalism was on hand to provide this ideology, it was partly because the 'rational' modern state, in alienating this colonial intelligentsia, had also helped to discredit some of the traditional world views to which it might have turned, and so created the need for new symbolic systems. Like the Anglo-Irish middle class, these men and women appealed for their legitimation to the people, able to rejoin the state only if it could be transformed into a nation. The common people thus found themselves wooed by two sets of suitors, from Young Ireland and the *DUM* to *Sinn Fein* and the Abbey Theatre.

········

Intellectuals in the modern sense are what Edmund Burke most feared: rootless, cerebral, emotionally anaesthetized figures who had cut loose from their traditional functions within church and state, and now formed a dangerously free-floating caste of professional sceptics bereft of all social anchorage.[12] Their commitment was to ideas rather than institutions, which – even if the ideas in question were by no means radical – was enough to pose a question mark over their political loyalty. Clinical rationalists of this kind are to be both mocked and dreaded: mocked because of their ineffectualness, their lofty remoteness from the common life;[13] dreaded because this spurning of popular pieties can lead to political revolution.

Such figures are at once pathetic and virulent, ludicrously out-of-touch and alarmingly partisan. For the English, they are typically French. Once the naked, unhoused intellect has cut adrift from sentiment, custom, the sensuous textures of things, it can soar to a transcendent standpoint which at least has the virtues of being politically harmless; but it can also turn the distance between itself and those sentiments into the space of critique. 'Theory', which has occupied this ground in our own time, can thus be attacked as both biased and bloodless. The charge that it is unfeeling rests, ironically enough, on a particular theory of feeling, for which the affections are always local, private, intuitive and unreflective. It also overlooks the fact that – at least as far as the political left goes – a 'rational' critique of feeling and value is made in the name not of the sovereignty of Reason, but of an alternative set of feelings and values.

Intellectuals are not, need one say, the monopoly of the political left. To trade in ideas is to risk overestimating their importance, so that even the most materialist of thinkers tend to betray a vein of spontaneous idealism. It is hard for intellectuals not to feel that values and beliefs take precedence over politics and institutions. By its very nature, intellectual work can enter into alliance with a right-wing ontology, so that History is seen as governed by Spirit rather in the way that the intellectual's ideas lie at the source of his material livelihood. It was in combat with this view – what one might call the spontaneous ideology of intellectual life – that Karl Marx's work first saw the light of day. Towards the end of the nineteenth century, the word 'intellectual' comes to signify a sublimely Olympian mind which sets its face firmly against practice. The writings of Matthew Arnold, in which practice is not so much disowned as deferred, are a way-station in this development. But the word was also being used to mean a member of the learned professions, like clerics, lawyers and physicians, along with scientists and academics. What had helped to redefine 'intellectual' as a self-regarding elitism or a professional speciality was the contrast of both with the commercial hack, as well as with more venerable Victorian notions of ideological leadership, the 'man of letters' and the popularization of knowledge. At just the same time in Ireland, however, it was the idea of the intellectual as man of letters, as populist *Gauleiter* or cultural commissar, which was being retrieved by the Gaelic Revival.

Even so, there are good reasons why so many intellectuals have been on the left. Since their working conditions include the need for free inquiry, they tend to rally to the defence of civic rights, a liberalism which can take a more radical turn in authoritarian conditions. And since the modern intellectual's relation to political power is mediated and oblique, it is easier for her to be critical of it. The group also have the leisure, social status and intellectual tools with which to do so. It is part of their stock-in-trade to suspect traditional shibboleths and instinctual prejudices, in which they have rather less professional investment than clerics or politicians. This may not in itself lead to political leftism: if the prejudices in question are politically enlightened ones, it is by identifying with them, rather than fending them off, that the intellectuals become progressive in their turn. But the more academic sort of intellectual finds it hard to credit that any prejudice can be enlightened. The disinterestedness of the free-wheeling modern intellectual is by no means simply bogus: having shed a good many of his traditional ideological functions, he can indeed sit looser to specific social interests. But the same displacement can involve the power to put a whole social order into question, which was hardly the role of the intellectuals before the Enlightenment. In any case, the meritocracy of modern societies allows men and women from modest social backgrounds to rise to prominence simply by virtue of their intelligence. There is therefore less need – though it happens often enough – for them to shed *en route* the social and moral values they inherit from their native communities. As far as the Irish go, Oliver Goldsmith would be one such example.

If Burke denounces the intellectuals, he does so as the finest Irish intellectual of his day. This, however, is more irony than contradiction, as Antonio Gramsci's celebrated distinction between 'organic' and 'traditional' intellectuals might allow us to see.[14] Burke is one of the first to name and excoriate a caste of intellectuals, but he does so because he writes as an exemplary 'traditional' intellectual confronting an unholy bunch of 'organic' ones. If the French revolutionary theorists are the spokesmen of a new social class in the process of assuming power, Burke castigates them as an intellectual apologist for the status quo. Here, however, one irony encloses another. For if Burke was so eloquent an advocate of traditional pieties and sentiments, it was in part because he was an Irish expatriate in England, a blow-in or parvenu from a nation where custom, tradition and piety were highly valued. They were, to be sure, customs and traditions not altogether hospitable to the British; but by an extraordinary feat of inversion, Burke transformed these spiritual resources of the colony into a passionate defence of its imperial masters.[15] Moreover, if he was the leading 'traditional' intellectual in Britain, he was an 'organic' one in Ireland, as an unswerving champion of its persecuted people. And in yet another ironic twist, some of the ideological weapons he brandished in the cause of crown and constitution were to be bequeathed to the later anti-British nationalist movements of his native land.[16]

The crossing of intellectual frontiers, and the bearing of ideas on a culture as a whole: if these are two typical features of post-Enlightenment intellectuals, then it is hardly surprising that colonial societies should have proved such a fertile seedbed for them. As far as the crossing of academic borders goes, the national question in nineteenth-century Ireland was to lead medics into archaeology, lawyers into political economy, political economists into education, historians into law and art critics into musicology, as the question of nationhood came to leave its mark on even apparently recondite disciplines like astronomy and geology, carving out a space in which the most varied pursuits could mingle. Antiquarianism – a dissident pursuit on the whole in Ireland, where remembering the past has been, unlike in England, largely a radical matter – is itself a *portmanteau* affair, comprising a wide range of disciplines from literature and archaeology to history and philology. What distinguishes the intelligentsia of Victorian Ireland is a remarkable versatility of mind.

To some extent, to be sure, this has less to do with nationalism than with a more primitive stage of what one might term the division of intellectual labour, one which was typical of Victorian England too. The Victorian 'man of letters', with his synthesizing, popularizing functions, was yet to yield ground to the professional sociologist or literary critic, and as a literary hack needed to be versatile simply to survive.[17] From Coleridge and Carlyle to Arnold and Ruskin, men of letters perform the generalist role of intellectuals, exercising a cultural leadership and moral authority which by the end of the century in England is being rapidly overtaken by the coterie magazine, the hermetic treatise, the specialist journal. Linking literature and politics, oratory and moral exhortation, these men lay claim to spiritual leadership in a society whose traditional governors are being gradually ousted by industrial capitalism. Like all 'general' intellectuals, they are stranded somewhere between academic and amateur, combining at their best the rigour of the former with the latter's indifference to professional demarcations. Ireland, of course, is still at the time a largely pre-industrial order; but its own ruling class of burghers and landowners is proving equally incapable of ushering it into modernity, so that from the Young Irelanders to the Revival the question of alternative intellectual leadership raises its head there too. Thomas Carlyle, man of letters and Victorian sage *par excellence*, could thus prove a potent influence on the Young Irelanders and Standish O'Grady.[18]

By the 1870s and 1880s, however, as T. W. Heyck points out, Shakespeare is ceasing to be a 'man of letters', which is what he was for the 1840s, as the term narrows from covering poets, historians, journalists, political economists and the like to professional periodical writing.[19] Only English literary criticism, from F. R. Leavis and I. A. Richards to George Orwell and Raymond Williams, will pass on the flame of an all-round intellectual humanism, at the risk of an embarrassing sociological amateurism. If society is now too complex for the man of letters, academic discourse is becoming too complex for society. An amateur intellectual humanism, however, survives rather longer in Ireland, where intellectuals are thinner on the ground, academies in short supply, the intellectual superstructure less elaborate and the division of intellectual labour rather less advanced.[20] According to Liam O'Dowd, 'humanistic [as against technical] intellectuals have predominated [in Ireland] against a background of nationalist struggle'.[21] Perhaps they were also so prominent because such cultural capital, in Pierre Bourdieu's phrase, accrues value through its rarity in a largely backward, uneducated society. While *fin-de-siècle* England bears witness to a steady

11

professionalization of intellectual life, with the birth of academic house-journals like *Mind*, *Notes and Queries* and the *English Historical Review*, the Irish Revival is finding a major role for the wide-ranging amateur intellectual, known for the most part as creative writers. And if English life is increasingly in the grip of a professional scholarship allergic to 'general' intellectuals, Ireland is breeding at just this time a Romantic humanism impatient with the sequestered mind of the academic.

If the authority of the English man of letters was being diminished among other things by the specialized research of the universities, Ireland had far fewer such seats of learning. Many of its leading intellectuals were not Trinity College dons but lay enthusiasts, professionals in one field propelled by a sense of political responsibility into another. As far as late nineteenth-century Trinity College goes, W. J. Mc Cormack observes that 'one cannot consider Salmon's provostship, or the published correspondence of the Shakespearean scholar, Dowden, without sensing a pathological withdrawal from the modern world, a disengagement of intellect from actual reality'.[22] Many of the country's foremost intellectuals had links with the college but were not actually on its payroll. W. E. H. Lecky, who ends up espousing a conservative 'Trinity' ideology, was nevertheless a man of letters rather than a don, a figure of the public sphere rather than of the quadrangle. Indeed, he enjoyed the distinction of turning down the Regius Chair of History at Oxford. As an eminently popular author and skilled synthesizer of others' opinions, Lecky aimed his work at the general educated reader, and in this sense performed the functions of the classical intellectual. He did so too in his ability to move from history, sociology and philosophy to religion, ethics and politics, as well as in his public political life as Member of Parliament for Dublin University. As far as the contrast between academics and intellectuals goes, it is significant that the chief organ of Anglo-Irish intellectual opinion, the *DUM*, had no official connection with Trinity College, staffed though it was by many of its alumni. It is true, even so, that the genteel-amateur humanism of the men of letters could become a mirror-image of the aesthetic trifling of the dons. John Pentland Mahaffy is perhaps best seen as a combination of the two.

If the sway of the English man of letters was also being usurped by the growth of a mass readership, which took its cue from the market rather than the sage, the backwardness of Irish publishing played its part in the survival of the public intellectual. Squeezed between market and university, despised by a professional intelligentsia for his eclecticism, partisanship and moral pretensions, and outflanked by the specialisation of knowledge, the English man of letters had fallen on hard times. The intricate division of intellectual labour which helped to drive him from the public sphere was itself a symptom of social crisis; but that crisis could only have been addressed by the very kind of intellectual humanist it was busy making redundant. However, while the end of the century in England saw the proliferation of purely literary reviews such as the *Savoy* or the *Yellow Book*, precious, exotic, hothouse growths which turned their back disdainfully on social questions, the same period in Ireland witnessed a major resurgence of cultural criticism.[23]

Nationalism, then, had a hand in the flourishing of the classical intellectual in nineteenth-century Ireland, as the state of the nation led thinkers from one scholarly discourse to another. Institutions like the Royal Irish Academy always had a distinctive 'national' ambience. As Liam O'Dowd has remarked, 'Specialist intellectuals come to have a much more prominent role in an intellectual stratum which is inclined to take cultural and national identity for granted'.[24] One might add that there is likely to be rather less tolerance for cloistered academicism in a society plagued by such urgent political problems. Yeats's well-aired scorn for Trinity College, which he none the less once applied to join, is exemplary of this impatience. Almost all of the major Irish intellectuals, for example – lawyers, novelists, clerics, political economists – turned their attention at one time or another to the politically fraught question of education. But the slow pace of academic professionalization in Ireland explains this intellectual all-roundness as much as nationalism does. John Anster, Irish translator of Goethe's *Faust*, also lectured on Roman civil law, while the interests of the celebrated Trinity wit John Pentland Mahaffy encompassed music, theology, Hebrew, modern languages, philosophy, ancient history, classical studies and cricket. As a classicist of world renown for his work on

Greek papyri, Mahaffy also published a brief monograph on Descartes, a work on Kant (praised by John Stuart Mill),[25] as well as a book on the rather more characteristic Ascendancy pursuit of trout fishing. He himself remarked of Trinity that 'manysidedness' had been a peculiar fashion of the College, perhaps a polite way of describing the incurable dilettantism of some of its dons. Like Oxbridge, Trinity tended to go in for a combination of heavy-duty scholarship and aesthetic frivolity, the latter providing some light relief from the former. Scholarship and frivolity are united in their distaste for utility. A typical example of scholarly trifling was the rather precious Trinity journal *Katabos*, edited by Arthur Palmer and Robert Tyrrell, which carried eruditely trivial pieces by Dowden, A. P. Graves, William Wilde, Thomas Rolleston, J. B. Bury and others.

The distinguished Trinity classicist Arthur Palmer produced a study of English horse-racing, while Alfred Perceval Graves remarked of the poet Samuel Ferguson that 'his very versatility rendered difficult that entire devotion to his art, of which Tennyson is the great modern example'.[26] Owen Dudley Edwards speaks of William Wilde as combining 'the Zenith of achievement of his time in demography, aural surgery, optical surgery, topography, ethnology, ethnography, medico-biography, public health and Irish character'.[27] Even the academic historian J. B. Bury, who was by no means a 'generalist', made a gracious concession to his Irish background by producing a life of St Patrick.[28] Isaac Butt was a typical Dublin jack of all trades: lawyer, novelist, translator, politician, political economist, political theorist.[29] The great Irish mathematician William Rowan Hamilton, a Kantian of sorts who had supposedly mastered Hebrew by the age of seven and some dozen or so other languages four years later, also preoccupied himself with poetry, theology, aesthetics and German Idealist philosophy. He won the Turner Prize for English verse, and was one of the founders of the science of optics as well as one of the mathematical geniuses of modern history. The railway pioneer James Pim associated with poets as well as with engineers and accountants. The political economist John Kells Ingram penned an essay on Shakespearean metre, and occupied a Chair in Oratory and English Literature, not political economy.[30] Patrick Kennedy, self-taught linguist and antiquarian, published nine novels and hundreds of

14

written-to-order periodical pieces. Arthur Houston, professor of political economy at Trinity, delivered a lecture on English drama.[31] W. K. Sullivan, who edited Eugene O'Curry's monumental tome *On the Manners and Customs of the Irish Nation*, was professor of chemistry at the Catholic University as well as a notable Celtic philologist.

Vivian Mercier writes of nineteenth-century Ireland's most exemplary intellectual, George Petrie, that he was 'Ireland's great nineteenth-century exemplar of Renaissance Man – painter, typographer, archaeologist, architectural historian, museum curator, and collector of folk music'.[32] Indeed, if Petrie was in some sense the Irish Ruskin, he was also rather more protean than his English counterpart, throwing in a few of the interests of a William Morris for good measure. Joseph Raftery comments in an essay on Petrie that in Ireland 'men in fields of scholarship have tended to venture into more than one area', and praises his subject, perhaps a mite prematurely, as 'the last of the great polymaths of Ireland'.[33] In late eighteenth-century Trinity College, it was not unusual to find a professor of Greek who was also held a chair of natural or experimental philosophy, and in the same era the scientist Richard Kirwan involved himself in chemistry, theology, metaphysics, mining, mechanics, geology, logic, law, music and meteorology, in the last of which he was a pioneer. Speaking before the British Association in Belfast in 1874, the Irish physicist John Tyndall reminded his scientific audience that 'The world embraces not only a Newton, but a Shakespeare – not only a Boyle, but a Raphael – not only a Kant, but a Beethoven – not only a Darwin, but a Carlyle'.[34] It is the typical ecumenism of the Victorian intellectual; but it also has a distinctively Irish resonance.

Writing in the journal *Atlantis*, W. K. Sullivan acknowledges the need for intellectual specialism but regrets the mutual isolation of the sciences, claiming that 'real intellectual progress requires the simultaneous advance of all kinds of knowledge'.[35] Indeed, in this particular essay Sullivan wants to pull together philology and the natural sciences, laying a kind of materialist or topographical basis for the science of sound. Upper-middle-class Irishmen locked into narrowly vocational pursuits like medicine or political economy, but who were also the heirs to a genteel-amateur ideology, could compensate for this lop-sidedness either by redefining their discipline in more generously humanistic terms, or by using it as a material base from which to launch some scholarly project of a quite different sort. Sir William Wilde did both, conceiving of his duties as a physician in broadly social terms, while using the wealth it bought him to delve into the treasures of Celtic antiquity. As Liam O'Dowd comments, such intellectuals 'may draw on a general moral or humanistic position or build outwards from their own specialities'.[36]

It is appropriate, then, that Dublin should have been, briefly and turbulently, the home of the Catholic University of John Henry Newman, one of Victorian England's most eloquent advocates of a humanistic as against a utilitarian education.[37] But if Newman's liberal humanism fitted in one sense with the ethos of the Irish intellectual, it was also a well-bred form of resistance to other aspects of Irish life. He writes in *The Idea of a University* of the need in Irish society for 'the force, the steadiness, the comprehensiveness, and the versatility of intellect' of which its 'intemperate and intractable' spirit, bred by sectarian rancour, has been deprived. 'Robbed, oppressed, and thrust aside, Catholics in these islands have not been in a condition for centuries to attempt the sort of education which is necessary for the man of the world, the statesman, the landowner, or the opulent gentlemen. . . . The time is come when this moral disability must be removed'.[38] The Irish mentality, in short, is hardly characterized by the Arnoldian virtues, and it is Newman's disconsolate mission to civilize the natives. There is, he considers, no greater calamity for a good cause than that the sectarians should get hold of it, a sentiment which might echo his own urbane wrangling over the disinterested ethos of the Catholic University with the ferociously interested Cardinal Cullen. 'The intellectual outlook of a sacristan' was how he scathingly described his episcopal opponent.[39] Archbishop John MacHale of Tuam returned the compliment, despising Newman simply because he was English. It was, in Arnoldian terms, a battle between Hellenist and Hebraist, and the Hellenists did not monopolize all the best arguments. Newman, who was not particularly interested in Ireland, saw the Catholic University largely in an English context, and as an academy for the Catholic upper class. He was also something of an absentee.

In characteristically high-minded style, and speaking as one of the earliest commentators on 'mass culture', Newman fears that the public sphere of disinterested debate, as we might call it after Jürgen Habermas, is in danger of being undermined by periodicals, popularization, instant communication, the trivial and ephemeral, all of which are conspiring to subvert the role of the universities. He speaks, that is to say, as one of Gramsci's traditional intellectuals, in opposition to what in the case of Ireland is the tendentious brawling of such journals as the *Nation* and the *Dublin University Review*. 'The authority, which in former times was lodged in Universities', Newman elegiacally notes, 'now resides in very great measure in that literary world'.[40] The traditional intellectual's faith in knowledge for its own sake is now being countered on one flank by the practically minded, socially engaged Anglo-Irish intelligentsia, and on the other by a Gaelic nationalism and Catholic moralism for which knowledge must be useful to be valid.

Newman, by contrast, looks to the university as an 'assemblage of learned men' who will create 'a pure and clear atmosphere of thought ... of which the attributes are, freedom, equitableness, calmness, moderation, and wisdom'.[41] The idea of a university, which for Newman himself is an eminently non-political notion, is little short of a full-blooded political alternative to Irish society, the upper-class English liberal's suave response to the squalid opinionatedness of a Daniel O'Connell. Newman, at least in public, praised the Irish as acute reasoners and subtle speculators, 'a people of great natural abilities, keen-witted, original and subtle', and observed that in medieval times 'philosopher' was almost the name of an Irish monk. Yet he also regarded his students as potentially 'disputatious, contentious, loquacious, presumptuous', which one would have expected on the whole to be complimentary rather than critical. While the English value the free play of the mind, the Irish perversely insist on arguing.[42] Newman's outlook is a fine instance of the liberal fallacy that only the view from nowhere is likely to elicit the truth – that specific interests are an obstacle to genuine understanding, rather than what might make it possible.

....

If prejudice can masquerade as disinterestedness in so noble a spirit as Newman's, it is hardly surprising that it does so in Irish intellectual life as a whole. Indeed, this conflict is implicit in the whole notion of the modern-day intellectual. Karl Mannheim sees the displacement of modern intellectuals, uprooted from their traditional social functions, as the basis of their dispassionate survey of social interests as a whole.[43] But such lordly dissociation, as we have seen already, can also clear a space for radical engagement. For some of this band, it is a matter of *reculer pour mieux sauter*. Those detached enough to glimpse something of the concealed logic of society may well find it in need of repair. Liam O'Dowd notes perceptively that if intellectuals 'claim to be the carriers of knowledge which transcends time, place and society', they also 'seek to demystify, to relativise and unmask'.[44] One might add that nationalist intellectuals tend to square this particular circle by raiding the resources of a 'timeless' national culture in order to unmask a highly specific colonial rule.

Even so, the tension between global disinterestedness and local partisanship remains acute. The chief task of an ethnic intelligentsia, comments Anthony Smith, is 'to mobilise a formerly passive community into forming a nation around the new vernacular historical culture that it has rediscovered. . . . Nationalism summons intellectuals everywhere to transform "low" into "high" cultures, oral into written, literary traditions, in order to preserve for posterity its fund of irreplaceable cultural values'.[45] But this, so to speak, is at once a global and partisan activity. The task of the 'organic' intellectual is to universalize, fusing the ideas of those she represents into a coherent whole; but the ideas themselves are antagonistic. For the nationalist intellectual, this paradox is writ large – for what she has to universalize are local pieties, regional affinities, stubbornly specific loyalties, all of which must be raised to theoretical respectability and furnished with an imposing historical pedigree. It is a tension captured by the slight but telling difference between 'nationalist' and 'national'. If the *Nation* was largely the former, the *DUM* saw itself chiefly as the latter. In one sense, perhaps, the nationalist intellectual is closer to the people than his Marxist counterpart, since what he articulates are less doctrines

18

than sentiments, less abstract theories than customary allegiances.[46] As Tom Nairn remarks, nationalism is 'constituted by a distinctive relationship between the intelligentsia (acting for its class) and the people', one which can be captured in the phrase 'intellectual populism'.[47] 'The new middle-class intelligentsia of nationalism', Nairn goes on, 'had to invite the masses into history; and the invitation-card had to be written in a language they understood'.[48] Here, then, is another reason for the Irish intellectual to beware of the esoteric.

Even so, recondite forms of scholarship which are carried on 'for their own sake' may in colonial conditions still carry an explosive political charge. The Revival found it easy enough to move between republicanism and Rosicrucianism. And in the curious doubleness of nationalist time, the most obscure excavations of the past can turn out to be urgently contemporary. It is this doubleness which Ernest Gellner has in mind when he remarks that nationalists tend to act like modernizers and talk like narodniks. Antonio Gramsci notes that 'a class some of whose strata still have a Ptolemaic conception of the world can none the less be the representative of a very advanced situation'.[49] The historian, antiquarian or archaeologist, bent on an unbiased account of the past, may by this very meticulousness come to unmask versions of it peddled by the colonialist, or supply nationalist artists with a world of imagery. Not all nineteenth-century scholarly 'revisionism' underwrote the status quo. The utmost scholarly rigour – George Petrie may provide an example – thus comes from time to time to be placed at the service of the people, as 'Culture' is linked with 'culture' in ways which Matthew Arnold could only dream of. Antiquarianism was both a respectable middle-class pursuit and a potentially subversive affair, whatever the reputable intentions of some of its practitioners. Petrie's renowned essay on Irish round towers is a piece of coolly demystifying demolition, as a set of outlandish theories of the towers' supposedly Danish, Persian, Phoenician or other exotic origin are efficiently despatched. Yet the effect of this soberly disinterested scholarship is to establish the towers as authentically Irish, and thus, whatever Petrie's own impeccably non-political motives, to lend power to the elbow of the cultural nationalists. Since he also dismisses the case that the early Irish were too barbarous to have constructed the towers, he compliments the nation in this sense too.[50] As Harry White points out, 'Petrie belonged to an Ireland in which antiquarianism had become so imbued with political resonance that the recovery of the past could not but signify immediate implications for the present'.[51]

Anthony Smith sees the nationalist intellectual as out to refine 'the community as a "nation" whose keys are unlocked [sic] by the "scientific" disciplines of archaeology, history, philology, anthropology and sociology'.[52] It is a rare conjuncture of high scholarship and popular sentiment. Even geology could be roped into its service, as the Geological Society of Dublin solemnly declared its intention to investigate 'the mineral structure of Earth, and more particularly Ireland', in the belief that its findings would be acceptable 'to the patriot and the man of science alike'.[53] As far as the social uses of knowledge go, the Trinity academic Samuel Houghton's *Principles of Animal Mechanics* (1873) was to have its enlightened public effects, as Houghton's researches led to the modern method of hanging by spinal dislocation rather than by strangling. It is an instructive instance of both the gains and limits of reformism.

It was convenient for the 'national' intellectual, then, that nineteenth-century Ireland had a politicized popular culture where culture in its 'higher' senses might occasionally find a home. Or, to put the point rather differently, culture in its broad, anthropological sense could provide a link between academic knowledge and the body politic. Art for Thomas Davis puts flesh on mere political facts, and thus moves men and women to political action; in this sense, it is the mediator between ideas and political life. Antiquarianism is for the most part history as culture, so that a pursuit which in other contexts would undoubtedly be the terrain of the traditional intellectual can pass into the hands of the organic one. If history is divisive, culture is unifying. Thomas Davis's celebrated *cri de coeur* to his fellow Protestant students at Trinity – 'Gentlemen, you have a country!' – is an invitation to traditional intellectuals to reconstitute themselves as organic ones. Scholarly restoration can thus mean political revolution, as the intellectuals provide a kind of cognitive mapping for political activists, often enough to their own dismay.

The line between history and politics, fact and fiction, has been blurred often enough in Ireland by the rewriting of history for rhetorical ends; but myth and legend are also legitimate objects of scholarly inquiry, fiction part of historical fact, and the findings of the academic can then always be pounced on by the politicians of the present. Nationalism thus provides a vital mediation between ideas and the common life, rather as art does for the Romanticism from which so much nationalist thought derives. The Romantic poet is out to abolish the elitist gap between artist and people by immersing himself in popular consciousness; but since he has already defined that consciousness as a source of superior wisdom, his own privileged status is deviously reinstated, without detriment to the common touch.

The nationalist intelligentsia, rather similarly, draws its authority from the masses which its own enabling fictions have constructed. The myths and images of the folk must be crystallized and cohered, but they are unlikely to do so under their own steam. To harness this culture to a political programme – a delicate enough task, to be sure, since Romantic nationalism has an allergy to the political as such – requires a fair amount of active intervention, which then threatens to re-open the rift between intellectual and people in the very act of seeking to close it. As Gellner remarks, the 'clerks' of nationalism are 'specialists yet more than specialists; they are both part of a society, and claim to be the voice of the whole of it'.[54] Like the *Nation* or the *DUM*, they seek to become representatives of the whole, ideal nation precisely by espousing a partisan cause. 'To act on a world', writes Thomas Davis, 'is for those *above* it, not *of* it'.[55] Or to put the dilemma in Thomas Duddy's terms, 'it is the problem of how to be sufficiently disengaged from the local culture to warrant being considered a member of the intelligentsia in the first place, while at the same time remaining sufficiently engaged with, or involved in, that culture to warrant being supported or at least tolerated by it'.[56] The difference is one between Karl Mannheim's 'free-floating' intellectual and Jean-Paul Sartre's *engagé* one. But the opposition is not so simple. Mannheim rejects the Gramscian notion of the organic intellectual, one who puts his or her talents in the service of particular social interests; but Sartre points to the

21

contradiction of those free-floating or traditional intellectuals whose skills 'are implicitly universalist, yet . . . are deployed according to the particular logics of capital and the state'.[57] We shall see something of this incongruity in the case of the nineteenth-century Irish intelligentsia, who were often enough 'state' intellectuals promoting a brand of universalist wisdom.

What needs resolving, then, is the 'disinterestedness' of the nationalist intelligentsia, concerned as they are with uniting different groups and classes under a single flag, and the obvious one-sidedness of this programme, at least from the standpoint of those it threatens. There is a similar tension in all intellectual work, since a respect for fact is itself, one might claim, a 'partisan' value. One can, after all, always ask *why* one should respect the facts, which Standish O'Grady – never an enthusiast for accuracy – implicitly did. Clarity, scrupulousness, honesty, judiciousness, patience, openness to revision: if these are among the ways in which the facts are established, they are also moral options in themselves. Intellectual work, and some at least of the liberal virtues, thus go hand-in-hand – though the scholar's suspicion of broad speculations, general theses and popular prejudices can also incline him to conservatism, even when the theses and prejudices in question are entirely justified. A prejudice against prejudice as such is a bias in itself, and a deeply unreasonable one.

The tension, however, is apparent on a broader scale too. It is one familiar enough in the writings of Thomas Davis, which veer from warm-hearted cultural inclusiveness to bellicose political invective. The writings of the more liberal Anglo-Irish insist on the need for an enlightened multiculturalism in a tone of urgency which is sometimes not far from the intensity of polemic, a genre in which the class was admirably proficient. If culture and politics are at odds for a Tory patriot like Samuel Ferguson, so they are for the nationalist Davis, who like Ferguson embraces the myth of culture as a solvent of social divisions.[58] But the strain is particularly obvious among the national-minded Anglo-Irish, whose liberal disinterestedness may have to stretch to the point where they find themselves excluded from the very political order they seek to establish. They must therefore find a way of appealing to the national culture which, by

22

treating it as the common ground upon which all the Irish may meet, succeeds in suppressing actual differences, as well as displacing attention from their own class privilege and counter-revolutionary politics. Culture must first be detached from society in order to rejoin it as an answer to its ailments.

This disinterestedness, however, is too flagrantly self-interested, and so threatens to be self-cancelling. For the Gaelic nationalists, culture is part of the political problem; for their Arnoldian Anglo-Irish counterparts, it can serve as a transcendent solution. The synoptic cultural vision of an organ like the *DUM* is finally at odds with its sometimes sectarian political agenda, so that as strident a Tory as the young Isaac Butt can, with scant sense of incongruity, echo Newman's appeal for a serene, elevated, even-handed public sphere of discourse which transcends all petty political strife. In a typically 'traditional' gesture, Butt complains that the growth of a valuable literature in Ireland has been thwarted by shallow sectarian attachments, and bemoans the lack of that 'spirit of refinement and severe good taste' which might 'correct, reduce, chasten, and harmonise the tumultuous and turbid exuberance of our unprincipled and random literature'.[59] But this venture in Irish Arnoldianism is itself, in a familiar Irish irony, marked by the very turbid exuberance it chastises: Butt writes of 'the miserable cant of a barbaric patriotism', along with 'the elements of wrath, and fury, and popular madness' in the country. Disinterestedness is thus imbued with all the rancour of the sectarianism it upbraids. Butt's appeal – one of several in nineteenth-century Ireland – is for that sphere of judicious public opinion which a fractious nation so fatally lacks. The Irish have no equivalent of Jürgen Habermas's *Öffenlichkeit*.[60] In fact they did, all the way from the United Irishmen to the Repeal movement and the Young Irelanders, all of whom fashioned a Habermasian public sphere of newspapers, reading-rooms, lectures, popular publications, the ceaseless circulation of discourse and the like. But these were *counter*-public spheres, which is not exactly what Isaac Butt has in mind.[61]

W. J. Mc Cormack contrasts the 'appearance of lofty elevation' of the *DUM* with the explicitly polemical stance of the *Nation*,[62] even though, as Mc Cormack points out, the former journal had

23

undoubted links with conservative politics. Michael Sadleir is rather less restrained, writing of the *Magazine*'s 'violent alternatives of savage partisanship, portentous solemnity, pert silliness and donnish pedantry', its contradictory mixture of the high-mindedly conservative and 'a college-boy enthusiasm on the loose'.[63] Thomas Davis is instructive on this contradiction, speaking of those Irish intellectuals 'who prized the oratory of Grattan and Curran, the novels of Griffin and Carleton, the pictures of Maclise and Burton, the ancient music, as much as any, and far more than most, of the political nationalists, but who regarded political independence as a dangerous dream. Unknowingly they fostered it. Their writing, their patronage, their talk was of Ireland; yet it hardly occurred to them that the ideal would flow into the practical, or that they, with their dead of agitation, were forwarding a revolution'.[64] In fact, it occurred to a good many of them; if they were sometimes disingenuous, they were rarely naive.

In any case, as Gaelic nationalism came increasingly to conquer the political sphere, culture became one of the few forms of politics which the 'national' Anglo-Irish could still hope to dominate. Having failed to provide the nation with political leadership, they now made an eleventh-hour strike for spiritual hegemony, devotedly restoring the national culture in ways which might have proved less necessary had some of their ancestors not sought so zealously to disrupt it.[65] The Ascendency had the wealth, guilt, leisure, intellectual training and sense of civic responsibility for just such a task; and the Revival would be the final apotheosis of this project, more or less redefining politics as culture. In the words of George Petrie, the common pursuit of ancient Irish culture would promote a 'national concordant feeling, in a country divided by religious and political discord.[66] Like all decent liberals, Petrie regarded this transcendence of politics as firmly non-political. Even so, the project was not entirely absurd in a colonial nation where culture meant less Dante and Schubert than language, religion, popular custom, ethnic identity. It was also more plausible in a colonial context where culture, as a common national heritage, cut across class rather more than it did in Britain. Disinterestedness could thus fare somewhat better in Ireland than in England, since the common ground sought after in the colony was the nation, rather than some vacuous Arnoldian universal. Such cultural 'universalism' is by no means just an illusion: ethnicity is indeed shared across classes, genders and vocations, a fact obvious not least when the nation is a reality still struggling to be born. But it proved rather less viable in an England for which culture meant, *à la* Arnold, sweetness and light or the best that had been thought and said.[67] Culture cannot provide the common ground of an industrial society whose major conflicts are those of class, since its own class-basis is far too obvious; it has a better chance of promoting itself in colonial conditions, where culture, in one sense at least, really is what you share in opposition to your ethnically alien rulers.

Despite all this, the Irish were to prefer the clergy to the clerisy. The efforts of English intellectuals to reinvent themselves as a spiritual elite, all the way from Young England to Bloomsbury, Coleridge's clerisy to Arnold's 'Remnant', were a just-plausible attempt to seize the high ground increasingly abandoned by the church in an era of rapid secularization. If the clergy could no longer provide such direction, then perhaps E. M. Forster's choice band of plucky liberal spirits, or Leavis's coterie of critics, could do the job instead. But the Irish already had a formidable spiritual leadership in those who, for Gramsci, are the most archetypal of traditional intellectuals: the Roman Catholic priesthood. And this group now found itself plunged into an uneasy alliance-cum-antagonism with yet another set of popular leaders: the organic intellectuals of nationalism, or as Anthony Smith dubs them, 'the new priesthood of the nation'.[68] Smith sees this new priesthood as arising from the ashes of the old: the medieval clergy, bastions of state power, give way to a more secular, humanistic intelligentsia in the Renaissance, who remain loyal to the state, and they in turn yield ground to the dissident intellectuals of the Enlightenment, ancestors of the radical clerks of modernity. The Anglo-Irish clerisy thus found itself doubly displaced, by both priest and politician. In his *Religious Tendencies of the Age*, W. E. H. Lecky considered intellectuals the priesthood of the modern world, taking his cue from his friend Thomas Carlyle's description of literature as the one modern church; but this group, so Lecky thought, was held back in Ireland by its lack of secularization.

From Isaac Butt to W. B. Yeats, the more enlightened of the Anglo-Irish had striven both selflessly and self-interestedly to transform themselves from a traditional to an organic intelligentsia – to relinquish some of their 'natural' affiliations to the colonial governing class, and place themselves instead at the service of the people. Or at least, if this proved too revolutionary a reinvention, to unearth some middle ground between the two. An elite was thus in the process of trying to convert itself into a vanguard, providing a solution to a problem which included its own political existence.

If the Anglo-Irish could strive for this role, it was partly because of a familiar division of labour between intellectuals and political activists. Those whose task is to run the revolution, with a few notable exceptions, rarely have the time to theorize about it. The utilitarian cast of much Irish nationalist thought, for which any knowledge not serviceable to the national cause was to be patriotically dismissed, was certainly one reason for the relative paucity of Irish intellectual life, even if that utilitarianism reflected the very English ideology which most Irish nationalists abhorred. In an essay on the nationalist tradition, Patrick Pearse tries rather forlornly to recruit Wolfe Tone, with his 'austere and piercing intellect', as a leading intellectual in a somewhat infertile Irish field. Only he, Davis, Fintan Lalor and John Mitchel, so Pearse glumly considers, have left a significant body of teaching behind them. Not many historians would concur with Pearse's judgement: Marianne Elliot sees Tone as 'a distiller of ideas rather than an original thinker', though she continues, a touch inconsistently, by pointing out the originality of his rejection of Lockean thought as undemocratic, since the social contract is tyrannically binding on subsequent generations. 'Tone's rejection [of Locke]', Elliott writes, 'represents a break with contemporary political philosophy far more fundamental than that of the philosophical radicals in England, with whom Tone otherwise had much in common'.[69] So perhaps he is not quite so derivative as she first imagined. Indeed, Thomas Bartlett boldly underlines what he sees as the originality of Tone's thought, seeing him as probably the first Irish separatist.[70] Tone was certainly a political pamphleteer more than a scholar, but this public, popularizing activity is part of the classical meaning of the term 'intellectual'. And though he may not have conjured his theories *ex nihilo*, his thought was nourished by the single most exciting ferment of ideas which modern Ireland has ever witnessed. This heady, intertextual brew of classical republicanism, civic humanism, Protestant Dissent, the Ulster and Scottish Enlightenments, Freemasonry, Paineism, American revolutionary notions, the Commonwealth men, Patriot clubs, Molesworth, Molyneux and the like far outstrips the Literary Revival in intellectual depth, daring and rigour. Anyway, quite what constitutes an 'original' body of thought has itself become problematic in some of the most original European philosophy of our own time.

Otherwise, however, Pearse's judgement is relatively sound. As far as the United Irishmen go, the owl of Minerva flew not at dusk but at dawn, as the politicos seized hold of enlightened republic notions which had long been in the making. Daniel O'Connell was not a theoretician: as with most great political strategists and rhetoricians, his writings were for the most part instrumental and *ad hoc*.[71] No one, Pearse remarks, 'gives O'Connell a place in the history of political thought'.[72] Robert Emmett's mind was 'great . . . but we have not its fruits'. Parnell, in Pearse's view, was 'less a political thinker than an embodied conviction', a man who disclaimed theories and confined himself to political practice.[73] Thomas Davis is said by Gavan Duffy to have wanted his name up with O'Neill, Tone and Grattan rather than Moore and Goldsmith, but whether his wish was fulfilled is dubious.[74] Indeed, the painful split displayed by the Young Irelanders between rhetoric and practice, high-sounding words and bungled actions, is one instance of a gap between theory and political action which typifies nineteenth-century Irish nationalism as a whole.

With due immodesty, Pearse might in fact have included his own enlightened, libertarian writings on education among the intellectual innovations of Irish nationalism; but his general case is surely valid. Until the time of James Connolly, it is hard to think of a single major theoretical treatise in the annals of Irish nationalist thought. No systematic critique of colonialism was to emerge. There are pamphlets, essays, novels, poems, histories, speeches from the dock or the hustings, but no body of sustained, significant theoretical work. The more politically *engagé* who might have produced it had scant leisure or resources to do so, committed as they were to texts which were practical, rhetorical, strategic. John Mitchel writes of Thomas Davis that '"literature", for the mere sake of literature, he almost despised'.[75] On the other hand, those who monopolized those intellectual resources often lacked the political motivation. The poorest in the country were also the most culturally deprived, and so bereft of the conceptual tools which might have helped to repair their condition. One of the most pathbreaking of Irish radical thinkers, William Thompson, who along with Edmund Burke is perhaps the greatest Irish intellectual at the turn of the eighteenth century, wrote on socialism and feminism rather than national-ism.[76]

Ernest Boyd puts this intellectual dearth down to the Catholic Church: 'Catholicism in Ireland', he writes, 'has been puritanical and inarticulate, and the task of fostering thought and education has naturally fallen to Protestants'.[77] Boyd is hardly an unpreju-diced commentator, and it is doubtful that popular Irish Catholicism (as opposed to the clergy) was always puritanical, let alone inarticu-late. But he is right even so to identify the Irish Catholic Church, a doughty antagonist of intellectual freedom, as one major reason why a theoretically ambitious Gaelic intelligentsia never emerged on the island. Sibling rivalry, Boyd might have added, was another such factor: the Catholic Church's fear of a secular, organic intelli-gentsia which would challenge its own sovereignty. Many of those who might have risen to intellectual prominence were siphoned off by the Maynooth seminary to staff the very institution which was most hostile to free inquiry. The Lord Lieutenant described Maynooth in 1844 as having 'more the air of a barrack than a national estab-lishment'.[78] W. E. H. Lecky regarded Catholicism as 'the most deadly enemy of the scientific spirit'.[79]

It is a sign of that hostility that the Irish Catholic Church, having set the intellectual pace for Europe in pre-modern times, was never to produce an original body of theology in the modern age. Theo-logy in Ireland was too blunt an instrument of apologetics to lend itself to nuanced intellectual inquiry. If the country played reluctant host for a while to the finest English theologian of the nineteenth century, John Henry Newman, it was never itself able to rival

28

Newman's luminous intellect and imaginative flair. Some of the most fascinating Catholic theology of nineteenth-century Ireland is dissident and heterodox, written against the grain of a lifeless scholasticism. The theological modernist George Tyrrell, disciple of Loisy and von Hugel and a brave advocate of church democracy, was excommunicated.[80] And Tyrrell can hardly be rated a theologian of the stature of a Newman, a Niebuhr or a Schleiermacher. Of course, the established church in nineteenth-century Ireland, with its evangelical, anti-intellectual cast, was scarcely a theological power-house either; but this was less because of intellectual autocracy than because it was a form of politics first and a religion rather a long way second. As Oscar Wilde remarked, he was an Irish Protestant, and so had no religion. Frank O'Connor declares in *The Backward Look* that no Irishman is of much interest until he has lost his faith, while the Anglo-Irish Gabriel Godkin remarks in John Banville's novel *Birchwood* that 'religion was regarded, like fox hunting, as nothing more than a ritual profession of the indestructibility of our class'. Even so, the traditional relation between Protestantism and free inquiry was to be one reason – their material and cultural privileges were another – for the prominence of the Anglo-Irish in the realm of artistic culture. Ernest Boyd remarks that there are many 'distinguished heretics' from Irish Protestantism in the nation's literary, political and religious life; indeed, he believes this to include 'almost every important Irishman in the literary history of the country'.[81] And George Moore was to become obsessively convinced that the very phrase 'Catholic novelist' was an oxymoron.

Nineteenth-century Ireland, in other words, is a striking illustration of Karl Marx's dictum that those who dominate the means of material production will also tend to control the means of intellectual production. That this is so is nowhere more evident than in the domain of artistic culture, which in Ireland follows the trajectory of class power with an exactness enough to embarrass even the most vulgar of Marxists. In the wake of the United Irish insurrection, the country produces its first 'national' poet, Thomas Moore. A little later, almost on the stroke of Catholic Emancipation in the late 1820s, Catholic writers (Gerald Griffin, John and Michael Banim) emerge for the first time as novelists, a literary sphere previously monopolized by the Ascendency. But Catholic hegemony in the novel is still not secure: the most distinguished nineteenth-century practitioner of the form, William Carleton, is a lower-class Catholic turned middle-class Protestant, as though eminent literary status still requires an alliance with the governing political Establishment. As it wins its partial independence, the nation gives birth to its supreme writer of fiction, James Joyce, a scion of the Catholic petty bourgeoisie which had spearheaded the political revolution. *Ulysses* and the Free State are born in the same momentous hour. If Irish Catholicism failed to generate an impressive theology, it nevertheless had a hand in the shaping of the finest Irish novelist.

Given the absence of a traditional Gaelic drama, however, it would still take some time for Gaelic-Irish authors to seize control in the theatre. In fact it is not until the 1950s that the first major dramatist of that provenance, Brendan Behan, will burst upon the scene, to be followed a decade later by the Ulster Catholic Brian Friel. About the same time, the struggle for civil rights in the North coincided with the flourishing of the greatest modern Irish poet, Seamus Heaney, as an increasingly articulate Catholic middle class in the province found both political and literary expression. Before then, the theatre had been firmly in the hands of Anglo-Irish Protestants, many of whom had 'exported' it to England: Farquhar, Goldsmith, Sheridan, Boucicault, Wilde, Shaw, Yeats, Synge, Lady Gregory, Denis Johnston, Samuel Beckett. Even Sean O'Casey was a Protestant – though this, one might claim, was something of a historical accident in the way that the Protestantism of Goldsmith or Yeats was not.[82]

....

What distinguishes Irish intellectual life in the nineteenth and early twentieth centuries is a massive displacement from the theoretical to the imaginative, or from the philosophical to the literary.[83] Far from confirming Gavan Duffy's prejudice that 'the Celtic temperament is averse to abstract studies',[84] this displacement sprang from particular historical conditions. Among them were the island's rich lineages of native literature, the material and educational disadvantages of the Gaelic population, the concern of their intelligentsia with immediate political struggle rather than with the *longue durée* of theoretical reflection, the Ascendency's effective monopoly of the means of intellectual production, along with their typically Anglo-Saxon distaste for ideas. It is thus that the true intellectuals of the United Irish epoch were novelists like Maria Edgeworth and Lady Morgan, anatomizing an entity known as 'Irish society' for the first time in fiction, rather than Lord Edward Fitzgerald or Robert Emmet. Vivian Mercier observes that, 'In truth, 1798 failed to inspire a single great work of imaginative literature, whether poem, drama, or novel',[85] though he overlooks Lady Morgan's finest novel, *The O'Briens and the O'Flaherties*.

Thomas Moore – poet, essayist, historian, satirist, political propagandist – marks the opening up of what might be called a Catholic public sphere of letters; he is an Irish man of letters in just the sense that, say, Thomas Carlyle or Leslie Stephen will be in England. Some of the most powerful political interventions of the period – the *Memoirs of Captain Rock* springs to mind – are thus, significantly, the work of a poet, just as Moore's twin poetic pieces *Corruption* and *Intolerance* are literary verse and political pamphleteering together. The 'political sociology' of the Emancipation period arises not from Daniel O'Connell but from John and Michael Banim, whose fiction is self-consciously an attempt to sketch for a sceptical British reading public the true lineaments of Irish society. In the absence of a 'totalizing' native sociology, this task will be inherited by William Carleton. It helped the Gaelic intelligentsia in this respect that you could become a creative writer with little formal education, as you could not so easily become, say, a philosopher or a physicist. The national schools were to be founded only in the 1830s,[86] after the first wave of militant nationalism, and were characterized by massive student absenteeism, untrained teachers, low salaries and a dismally unenlightened curriculum, with fuel and books provided often enough by parents and building repairs by teachers.[87] The Catholic University was a failure, Trinity College still placed restrictions on Catholic students, while the Queen's Colleges, established in the 1840s, fell under the anathema of the Catholic hierarchy. The quality of their students was in any case extremely poor, well below

English standards. In 1836–7, the country had only 1300 schools for a population of around eight million, and a few years later over half that population was reported to be illiterate.[88]

The Irish novel, then, becomes for better or worse an *ersatz* form of sociology, at once intimate and objectifying, inward and distancing. Just as Balzac had been the supreme 'sociologist' of post-revolutionary France, so Ireland stood in need of a similar form of totalization through imaginative fiction – at least in the view of the novelist James Stephens, who complained that 'We lack a mirror, a synthesis, we cannot see ourselves', and yearned to pen a kind of *Comedie Humaine* of his native land.[89] Before sociology proper arrives on the scene, an event which in Ireland might be dated from the writings of the Comtean John Kells Ingram, the novel can do service for it. Even poetry can provide an alternative: William Allingham caustically described his poem *Laurence Bloomfield in Ireland* as 'The Landlord and Tenant Question in flat decasyllables'.[90] And if poetry could be sociology, history could be literature: W. E. H. Lecky records his opinion that 'there is no subject in which rarer literary qualities are more demanded than in the higher forms of history'.[91] The *DUM*, more a political than a literary organ, was edited for a while by a novelist, Charles Lever, who never seemed to have had an idea in his head. It was also a novelist, Sheridan Le Fanu, who took over the editorial chair of the *Dublin Evening Mail*, to articulate the interests of the Protestant elite. For a while, Le Fanu was also proprietor of the *DUM*.

But the literary can be a placeholder for the social only for so long. Once the idea of underlying social laws begins to surface, of structures and forces whose logic is relatively independent of individual lives, the novel form, which depends on the translatability of social facts into interpersonal terms, or (as with so-called Irish Protestant Gothic) into emotional scenarios, can no longer really cope. Literary realism is accordingly plunged into crisis: George Eliot's *Middlemarch* represents perhaps the last point in English society when it still seems possible, in Shelley's phrase, to 'imagine what we know', to flesh out the complex laws of social life as palpable human drama. The object of social knowledge is now becoming invisible, as it will soon be in psychology too; and this will require a

32

new division of intellectual labour, in which a professional sociology or anthropology takes care of those structures invisible to the artistic eye, leaving literature as the domain of the seen, heard and handled. At the end of the century, the literary naturalism of a Zola or George Moore seeks to restore literature's cognitive status by miming the scientific spirit, converting the novel itself into a form of clinical sociology; but the experiment will prove short-lived, as imaginative writing retreats increasingly to the realm of the inward and subjective, leaving the more socially minded disciplines to dominate the field of public affairs. It is thus that the basis for modernism is laid down.

If literature in nineteenth-century Ireland was to become a form of social or political critique, Young Ireland reversed the terms to superb effect, producing political propaganda which ranks among some of the finest imaginative writing of the century.[92] James Fintan Lalor, Thomas Meagher and John Mitchel were all superlative stylists; indeed, William Dillon observed in a notably back-handed compliment that Mitchel should have stuck to literature, while Lalor's editor Lilian Fogarty considers that his style alone, which to her mind recalls Swift, Berkeley and Burke, is enough to secure his place in the national literary pantheon.[93] A similar substitution of the poetic for the political is true of the Revival, run by a specifically literary intelligentsia who were intellectuals in the broad scope of the word, but scarcely theoreticians. Only Synge stands out as an intellectual in the strict sense, with his impressively wide reading: Dante, Spinoza, Taine, Hegel, Lessing, Schlegel, Marx, Darwin, Nietzsche, William Morris, most of the French classical authors.[94] In the typical style of the Irish intellectual, his interests also encompassed musicology, philology and the natural sciences.

Some other Revivalists, by contrast, drew their materials from a writer who was really a poet masquerading as a scholar, Standish O'Grady.[95] As a mediator between the academics and the artists, treating history in ways which made it available for art, O'Grady fulfilled something of the role in Ireland of the English man of letters. 'Archaeology culminates in history, history in art', was his slogan.[96] History is the conduit by which past myth passes into present culture, in what amounts to a four-stage translation: myth encodes the history of the people; the modern historian retrieves the myth, which the artist then deploys for public ends, thus restoring it to the people. The history of one generation, O'Grady writes in his *Introduction to Early Bardic Literature*, becomes the poetry of the next, and for him the conversion is all the simpler since the history was really poetry all along. As an Irish equivalent to the Diltheyan school of historical empathy in Germany, his *History of Ireland: the Heroic Period* (1878) rejects any objectivistic historiography and wants instead to reconstruct the 'imaginative processes' of the past. His mission is to make this early Irish history 'once again a portion of the imagination of the country', supplying Irish nationalism with its fables and symbols rather as Milton had done for the English revolution and William Blake for the industrial one. He had a Carlylean impatience with analytical thought, just as Sean O'Casey had a prolier-than-thou contempt for its social privilege.

O'Grady, who though not great himself was the cause of greatness in others, thus marks the point where historical scholarship becomes a handmaiden to art, despite his lofty disapproval of the Revivalist theatre which drew on his fund of legends. The balance between academic and creative writing is now shifting decisively towards the latter, as the major imaginative works which were never forthcoming from Young Ireland begin to appear. Young Ireland had more practical preoccupations, while with a handful of exceptions (Charles Lever, Samuel Ferguson) the mid-century Ascendancy intelligentsia produced scholars and men of letters rather than literary artists. With the Revival, however, the Ascendancy now comes to dominate the field of literature too, once a previous generation of saga-hunters and myth-collectors has turned up the scholarly soil for it. As the political temperature rises from the Land League onward, a rising nationalist class has need of its symbols and legitimating histories, and it is the role of their Anglo-Irish superiors to provide them.

Besides, having chalked up some political victories, nationalism is now buoyant enough to engage in a little self-reflection, striking beneath political questions to the layers of poetic and philosophical meaning sedimented beneath them. As with all emergent classes, in Gramsci's view, it needs a world view as well as a political pro-

34

gramme. An Anglo-Irish coterie with a natural penchant for spir-itual inquiry, as well as with the leisure and cultivation to pursue such matters, can thus seize upon culture partly to compensate for its growing political marginality. Like warfare, culture is politics by other means, at once a deepening and a displacement of the strife on the Dublin streets. The intellectual background to the Revival is less sociology than theosophy.[97] George Bernard Shaw, who was every conservative's nightmare of a desiccated intellectual, might be said to have reversed the shift from theory to the imagination, producing at his worst a range of cerebral treatises thinly disguised as plays. (Though Shaw's unabashed intellectualism can also be seen as a strike at English philistinism and sentimentalism, just as Wilde deployed a hard-boiled wit and dazzling play of mind for much the same ends. To this extent, the absence of a strong liberal humanist heritage in Ireland, debilitating in other ways, could at least be exploited to puncture the sentimental humanism of its colonial masters.)[98]

....

The link between nationalism and the intellectuals is clearly more than a matter of scholarly flexibility. In the modern epoch, 'culture' in its broad, anthropological sense becomes one means by which an atomistic social order can be held together; and it is thus hardly surprising that the organizers of that field – intellectuals – should assume a higher profile.[99] Culture, at least on one influential theory, comes to act as a central means of social communication once pre-modern social structures have been loosened up. If tribal bonds, feudal fealties or an absolutist state can no longer hold a people together, a common language, education and belief-system might serve instead. And since culture is the very medium of nationalist struggle, it is hardly surprising that intellectuals should play a more activist role in colonial societies than in metropolitan ones. In their markedly different ways, both Ernest Gellner and Benedict Anderson see nationalism as facilitating and facilitated by culture.[100] It is not only that intellectuals play a conspicuous part in the movement; it is also that certain cultural developments – spreading literacy, a common language, a universal educational system – are among the conditions for political nationalism as such. Elie Kedourie, rather gnomically, describes nationalism as 'the invention of literary men'.[101] As Anthony Smith has observed, 'The intelligentsia always contributes representatives [to national movements] out of proportion to its numbers, if by "intelligentsia" is meant lawyers, journalists, academics, doctors and teachers, and all who possess higher educational qualifications'.[102] Smith's list of professionals is precise in the case of Ireland: Daniel O'Connell and Isaac Butt (lawyers), John Mitchel, Charles Gavan Duffy, Arthur Griffith and D. P. Moran (journalists), William Wilde and William Stokes (doctors), Eoinn Mac Neill and Thomas MacDonagh (academics), Patrick Pearse (teacher).

In other ways, however, these men are a mixed bunch, ranging from the traditional 'genteel' professions (law, medicine, academia) to functionaries of the modern state and media. To some extent, this difference corresponds to Gramsci's distinction between traditional and organic, a distinction which is less one of social origin than of social function.[103] As far as social origin goes, hardly any of the organic intellectuals of the national movement before Michael Davitt and James Connolly stemmed from the people.[104] Fintan Lalor, sometimes idyllically seen as a 'peasant', was in fact the son of a County Laois middleman who held over one thousand acres. Indeed, Gramsci himself argues that 'the mass of the peasantry . . . does not elaborate its own "organic" intellectuals', though a high proportion of traditional intellectuals are of peasant origin.[105] This is true in a sense of Ireland, where the son of a 'peasant' was far more likely to join that group of traditional intellectuals known as the clergy than to whip up political revolt. But 'peasant' here would be an overstretched term: the great majority of the Irish clergy were drawn not from the small tenantry or labourers but from the middle and strong farming classes.

The traditional/organic opposition, then, concerns less where you come from, or what vocation you follow, that what you do. For Gramsci, intellectuals are to be categorized less by the nature of their disciplines than by their function within sets of social relations. Just as various academic pursuits offer themselves at different times as the locus of the broader, more politically charged activity of the intellectual, so that even the humble sciences of geology and biology could come to play this role in religiously fraught Victorian England, so the organic intellectual is distinguished from her traditional counterpart by her 'active participation in practical life, as constructor, organiser, "permanent persuader", and not just as simple orator'.[106] On this view, Daniel O'Connell, Thomas Davis and Charles Stewart Parnell would qualify as organic Irish intellectuals, in contrast with, say, John Wilson Croker or James Joyce. The organic intellectual is a political leader as well as a specialist, though the category can also be used to include the state intelligentsia as a whole, whose scientific, administrative and political functions put them at odds with traditional intellectuals like artists, academics and philosophers. These men and women move at a greater distance from the public sphere, and the part they once played in politics and public service dwindles rapidly once a centralized, professional state bureaucracy begins to emerge. For Gramsci, it is precisely because these figures have a more mediated relation to political power and material production that they fall for the myth of the autonomous intellect. Thinkers who research in All Souls are more likely to imagine that their ideas are born purely of other ideas than those who work in advertising agencies. They thus serve the established order exactly by their apparent lack of dependence upon it, which then lays the material basis for liberal disinterestedness and idealist philosophy. Organic intellectuals, by contrast, exist only in vital relation to a specific class or group, as their 'thinking and organising element'.[107]

The role of these figures is to draw the fragmentary consciousness of those they represent into coherent, intellectually articulate form, equipping them with a 'world view' definitive enough to match that of their political antagonists. It is, in short, a secular version of what the Catholic clergy have done in both Italy and Ireland, and its model is secretly theological. Lady Wilde, once a member of the organic intelligentsia of Young Ireland, puts the point with Gramscian precision: 'The utterances of a people, though always vehement, are often incoherent; and it is then that men of education and culture are needed to interpret and formulate the vague longings and ambitions of the passionate hearts around them'.[108] 'A human mass', Gramsci writes, 'does not 'distinguish' itself, does not become independent in its own right without, in the widest sense, organising itself; and there is no organisation without intellectuals, that is without organisers and leaders . . . the existence of a group of people "specialised" in conceptual and philosophical elaboration of ideas'.[109] This is clearly true of the Irish nationalist movement from Tone to Connolly. The Young Irelanders would be a classic instance of Gramsci's 'national-popular' intellectuals, linking ideas and the common people, popular consciousness and the political state. But a figure like Davis, with his Romantic anti-utilitarianism, could just as well be seen as a traditional intellectual displaced by a rationalizing colonial state, and something of the same might be claimed of John Mitchel. There is much that is (in Gramsci's sense) traditional about the revolutionary vanguard of Young Ireland, whose abortive insurrection was to be led by the aristocratic, English-educated William Smith O'Brien.

One of the most vital tasks of an organic intelligentsia, according to Gramsci, is to assimilate the traditional intellectuals. For him, every social group tends to produce its own intellectuals, but 'those of the historically progressive class . . . exercise such a power of attraction that, in the last analysis, they end up by subjugating the intellectuals of other social groups'.[110] It is, on the whole, a job which Irish nationalism carried out remarkably well, hijacking in turn Wolfe Tone, Thomas Davis, Charles Stewart Parnell and W. B. Yeats. It is thus by no means the case, as Sean O'Faolain rashly claims in his *King of the Beggars*, that the Anglo-Irish contributed nothing to the rise of the common people.[111] On the contrary, their contribution was massive and enduring. There were plenty, however, who travelled the other way, abandoning their lower-class Catholic background to join the Protestant establishment. William Carleton was one; another was the Platonist philosopher Thomas Maguire, who started life as a Catholic, became a polemical Unionist and was involved in the anti-Parnell 'Pigott letters' forgery.[112]

The bearing of Gramsci's distinction on the group of patriots clustered around the *DUM* is rather more problematic. In one sense, these figures are clearly traditional intellectuals: poets, novelists, clerics, academics and the like, along with a sprinkling of the more venerable vocations of lawyer and physician (though lawyers also played an important role in the Repeal Association and the Irish Confederation). As such, they are at odds with the state intelligentsia of a reforming colonial power, which is threatening to modernize them out of existence from above, as well as at daggers drawn with the nationalist ideologues who are undercutting their power base from below. But as a militantly self-conscious intelligentsia rather than a set of solitary intellectuals, they also act as the spiritual organizers of their besieged social class, and can thus be described as 'organic' to it. Indeed, it is precisely because that Anglo-Irish class is now under fire that it is both possible and necessary for it to rise to such elaborate self-reflection. The role of its intellectuals is to lend it an agenda and identity in troubled times, when the Ascendancy gentleman can no longer take his existence spontaneously for granted.

The very emergence of the *DUM* thus marks a spiritual crisis in the fortunes of those it seeks to mobilize, as the odious Whigs force the good burghers of Victorian Dublin increasingly to the wall. Its strategy, even so, is far shrewder than the Revival's, which appealed over the heads of the middle class to an idealized populace who rarely showed up at the Abbey Theatre. By grooming the Anglo-Irish leadership rather than playing directly to the masses, the *DUM* can muster its troops for hegemony over the Catholic masses. Indeed, Samuel Ferguson manages to makes it sound as though the members of the Ascendancy have so far selflessly resisted all blandishments to wrest such dominion from the nationalists: 'with strong temptations to the gratification of selfish ambitions by assuming their natural place as leaders of the Irish masses', they have devoted themselves instead to science, letters and arts.[113] It is the equivalent of shunning a party to which you were never invited. Yet this function will only be fulfilled if the Ascendancy intelligentsia, or at least the more enlightened spirits among their ranks, can incorporate the nation as a whole into their self-refashioning, identifying their own destiny as a class with its corporate well-being. It is a far cry from the days of Swift and Flood, when the Anglo-Irish sometimes identified the whole of the Irish people with themselves; instead, they must now make common cause with a nation which is clamouring to overturn their sovereignty. How far they succeeded in doing so will be one of the themes of the chapters which follow.

2

Portrait of a Clerisy

In some memorable pages in his study of Leslie Stephen, Noel Annan writes of the 'emergence of an intellectual aristocracy' in Victorian England, as 'certain families establish an intellectual ascendancy and begin to share the spoils of the political and academic worlds with their children'.[1] The children, accustomed to hearing their parents discuss abstract questions with their friends, often choose for their own marriage partner the daughter or son of one of their father's circle, whose tastes and fortune are similar to their own. So it is that the great intellectual dynasties of nineteenth-century England – Macaulays, Trevelyans, Huxleys, Stephens, Arnolds and the like – come to reproduce themselves down the generations, forming a tight-knit network of 'able men and women' who in turn draw into their orbit men and women of intellectual distinction, and whose rambling Victorian homes thus act as a series of public spheres in miniature.

What is at stake here is what one might call a socio-intellectual formation, in which breeding and intellect, blood-ties and affinities of spirit, are hard to distinguish. The great sprawling families of the Victorian intelligentsia become informal academies in themselves, complete with tutors and students, masters and acolytes, scientific uncles and philosophical cousins. Something of the same cross-breeding of the domestic and the intellectual was to crop up in a different guise with the Bloomsbury group, that bohemian vanguard of early twentieth-century England which was always, according to its doyen Leonard Woolf, 'primarily and fundamentally a group of friends'.[2] The group had Cambridge as its unofficial background just as the *DUM* had Trinity, and there is more than a touch of Oxbridge in its patrician assumption that ideas and personalities are as inseparable as port wine and walnuts. It is the Platonic ideology of the traditional Oxbridge tutorial, for which talk of books flows as naturally from personal friendship as a stroll through the shrubbery. In its very English way, Bloomsbury had in Virginia Woolf's view 'no common theory, system or principles',[3] matters which could be left to self-made men or political fanatics; she did not add, because she did not see, that as a mildly dissident fraction of the English governing class, leashed tight to the very Establishment it satirized, it had no need of them. Made up of the epicene sons and mutinous daughters of the ruling patriarchs, it could never quite resolve its Oedipal ambivalence towards its oppressive elders.

For all their obvious differences, there is some parallel between Bloomsbury and the *DUM* coterie, as there is an obvious affinity between Annan's English intellectual dynasties and the equally incestuous *ménages* of Victorian Dublin. William and Jane Wilde would have had no problem at all in fitting into Bloomsbury. The Anglo-Irish cabal around the *DUM* was an earnest, high-minded, self-consciously political fraction, in contrast with the Bloomsburyites' flamboyant aestheticism; in this sense, the latter resemble the Wildes' prodigal son rather more than they do the class from which he sprang. Yet both coteries were the deviant intellectual wings of a military, professional, landowning upper class, even if this in the case of Bloomsbury took the form of a liberal progressivism, and with the *DUM* a radical conservatism. The *DUM* writers were out, as Clive Bell and Lytton Strachey were not, to recall their own class to its civic responsibilities; but to do that meant putting a toe behind the dull burghers of Dublin, as Young England was to do behind its own governing powers.

Both Bloomsbury and the *DUM* combined a sympathy for underdogs with a *de haut en bas* attitude to them, and something of what

Raymond Williams has to say of the former applies also to the latter: 'a fraction of an upper class, breaking from its dominant majority, relates to the lower class *as a matter of conscience*: not as solidarity, not in affiliation, but as an extension of what are still felt as personal or small-group obligations'.[4] If the bad conscience and evangelizing zeal of Protestantism lurks behind the Victorian Anglo-Irish, as it has been shown to inform the very name of the Irish Literary Revival,[5] much the same can be said of the Bells and Woolfs, whose spiritual elitism takes the form of a secular priesthood. There is a blending of high spirits and the high moral ground in both camps. If the Anglo-Irish reformers were not exactly Bloomsburyite free spirits, scornfully rejecting social convention for an anarchic lifestyle, they could nevertheless live it up libidinally behind their Georgian porticoes, as the scandal-ridden careers of Isaac Butt and William Wilde graphically illustrate. It is just that Bloomsbury wore insolently on its sleeve what some of the Anglo-Irish would have paid good money to conceal. What was a practice in Merrion Square became a theory in the precincts of the British Museum. Both circles were a curious cross-breed of elite and vanguard, and both grew out of what Williams describes in the case of Bloomsbury as certain changes in the professional and cultural life of the bourgeoisie, with the emergence of 'a new and very important professional and highly educated sector of the ... upper class: very different in its bearings from either the old aristocracy or from the directly commercial bourgeoisie'.[6] Williams speaks of the Bloomsbury group as having 'a significant frequency of connection with the upper levels of colonial (usually Indian) administration',[7] a connection reflected to some extent in Anglo-Irish Dublin. Whitley Stokes Junior, son of Sir William Stokes, was an Indian civil servant of remarkable distinction, awarded the highest honours in India.

John Butler Yeats's *Early Memories* underlines the affinity. Yeats contrasts what he sees as the repressive commercial middle-class milieu of his kinsfolk's Sligo with an idealized portrait of Dublin as the home of a blithe Hellenism, in which 'we ridiculed and criticised each other with great freedom, and with French malice'.[8] If this sounds Bloomsburyish enough, so does Yeats's portrayal of Dublin as a community which believed in 'parental affection and in conjugal faith and loyalty between friends', the conjugal faith apart.[9] 'We were a city without rules', he writes with an eye on Fitzwilliam Square rather than the Liberties. 'We lived for society and worshipped its pleasant needs, and for reward we had our social conceit'.[10] Like Bloomsbury, however, this gregarious impulse involves the flourishing of individuals rather than their sacrifice to social mores, and, in a hedonism Lytton Strachey would have approved, 'the master desire was for enjoyment'. Yeats captures the vaguely anti-commercial ethos of an intellectual rather than mercantile middle class ('Commerce is war, each man watching to take the bread out of his neighbour's mouth'),[11] a Bloomsbury-like distaste for low-bred business rather than a critique of capitalism.

If Yeats's middle-class Dublin could be described as a socio-intellectual formation, it is because its intellectual dealings were peculiarly face to face. As a group under political siege, its consciousness of itself as a class was naturally intensified: it was in the classical sense a bourgeoisie, a 'social force with its own sense of collective identity, characteristic moral codes and cultural *habitus*'.[12] Yet it was also dissolved into a network of interpersonal relations, along with an exotic cult of personality. Leinster House, sold by its aristocratic owner to the Dublin Society, became a cultural nucleus in the second half of the nineteenth century, an equivalent of the eighteenth-century London coffee house. Like Victorian London, Dublin was dominated by a handful of intellectual dynasties: Sheridans, Le Fanus, Wildes, Stokes, Graves, Hamiltons, Trenches, Balls.[13] Intellectually speaking, the capital was a small village, as it was still to be a century later in the days of the notoriously bibulous triumvirate of Brendan Behan, Patrick Kavanagh and Flann O'Brien. A few close-knit individuals could thus define an entire culture. A minuscule intelligentsia in a small colonial capital were likely to trade their ideas over dinner, conjoining two forms of oral activity. They were also a strikingly precocious set: Isaac Butt won Trinity's Whately Chair of Political Economy at the age of twenty-three, while the remarkable William Rowan Hamilton wrote a Syriac grammar at the age of twelve. Robert Kane was elected to the Chair of Chemistry of the Apothecaries' Company while still a Trinity undergraduate, and the 'Astronomer of Armagh', Thomas Robinson, wrote a volume of poetry at the age of twelve.

Like Annan's English intellectual caste, they were often each other's kinsfolk. Sheridan Le Fanu's paternal grandmother was a sister of Richard Brinsley Sheridan, and the Sheridans and Le Fanus were related by three different alliances. Oscar Wilde played as a child with Le Fanu's children, as he played on the beach at Dungarvan with a child who was later to prosecute him for buggery, Edward Carson. The word in Dublin was that Carson was wreaking his revenge on Oscar for having knocked over his sandcastle. Jane Elgee, Oscar Wilde's mother, was the great granddaughter of an eminent Dublin physician who had been a friend of Swift. The novelist Charles Maturin was the grand-uncle of Oscar Wilde; Henry Stokes, brother of the celebrated Sir William, married the sister-in-law of the Trinity wit John Pentland Mahaffy; while C. S. Stanford, co-founder of the *DUM*, married the granddaughter of Lord Edward Fitzgerald. Aubrey de Vere's sister was married to William Smith O'Brien's brother, and George Bernard Shaw's wife was the cousin of the novelist Edith Somerville, who thought Shaw rather low-bred. As for their intellectual intimacy, William R. P. Graves organized readings of Shakespeare attended by William and Marget Stokes, Ferguson, Dowden, Ingram, Mahaffy, Salmon and a range of other Anglo-Irish luminaries, who doled out the parts of plays like *Cymbeline* among themselves. The novelist Charles Lever gathered a circle of intellectuals around him at his Dublin home Templeogue House, while Lady Wilde's literary salons were legendary. Yeats put in the occasional appearance there. Lady Wilde's son Oscar loyally remarked of a rival Society hostess that in trying to launch a literary salon, she succeeded only in opening a restaurant.

It was an intellectual *Gemeinschaft* which to a large extent cut across political divisions in an otherwise fractious society. Blood, class and national sentiment proved thicker than politics, as John Mitchel played host to Samuel Ferguson and William Carleton along with his Young Ireland colleagues,[14] while W. E. H. Lecky and Gavan Duffy were close friends, and the nationalist Duffy always spoke sympathetically of the Tory Sheridan Le Fanu. Oscar Wilde remembered John Mitchel and William Smith O'Brien at his father's dinner table. A good many Protestant conservatives, including the curmudgeonly Le Fanu, spoke warmly of the *Nation*, while that journal made every effort to foster good relations with the *DUM*. John Mitchel writes of Thomas Davis in his *The Last Conquest of Ireland (Perhaps)* that he was 'no mere revolutionist' but a most welcome guest both at antiquarian reunions at the Royal Irish Academy and in the gay drawing-rooms of Dublin. Despite his supposedly incendiary politics, hardly anyone seems to have had a bad word to say about Davis, in a community where character and personality frequently counted for more than doctrine. William Dillon comments that Davis 'had everything to lose and nothing to gain by taking the popular side',[15] but if Mitchel's account is true his apostasy seems not to have banished him from fashionable *soirées*. Isaac Butt and Thomas Davis, both nationally minded lawyers, had much more in common than their stance on the national question would suggest. Sir Samuel Ferguson considered Davis 'a gentleman of most unaffected charming deportment', who speedily became 'the friend and favourite of the *elite* of the intellectual world of Dublin'. Lady Ferguson adds her own social compliments: 'Mr. Davis was by birth a gentleman, and both in feeling and in judgement opposed to all designs for destroying the legitimate power of the gentry'. He had no desire, she writes, to reduce the whole of society to one base level of peasants.[16] A little matter like anti-colonialism was clearly not going to jeopardize the bond between gentlefolk. As W. J. Mc Cormack puts it, 'In the Anglo-Irish scheme of things class could be discounted when it was inconvenient'.[17]

Lady Ferguson also commends William Smith O'Brien as 'a gentleman of birth and position. He was a brother to the late Lord Inchiquin, and was a man of fine presence and of chivalrous honour'.[18] His insurrectionary march around Tipperary is made to sound rather like an episode from the Arthurian legends. John Mitchel detested his fellow nationalist Daniel O'Connell ('the worst enemy I ever had') far more than he did some of those most hostile to his politics. The conservative landowner William Gregory, by contrast, who was responsible for the notorious 'Gregory clause' which resulted in Famine evictions, had a warm relationship at one time with his fellow landlord O'Connell.[19] Caste solidarity generally overrode political contentions: a committee established to secure a state pension for the widow of John Banim included O'Connell, William

Smith O'Brien, John Anster, Sheridan Le Fanu, Gavan Duffy, Isaac Butt, Charles Lever, Thomas Davis and Samuel Ferguson. Smith O'Brien, who headed the Young Ireland insurrection of 1848, was an affectionate correspondent of the virulently anti-democratic Catholic reactionary Aubrey de Vere. They were not a caste impervious to the lower-bred parvenu, as the careers of Carleton and Mangan, both of whom wrote for the *DUM*, would suggest; but there were limits to this clubbability, as we shall see later.

It was not a particularly prosperous community. Even though a Dublin maidservant in the 1870s cost only seven pounds a year, 'there were many families living a little over subsistence level who in point of culture were on a level with the well-to-do'.[20] As president of the Royal Irish Academy, William Rowan Hamilton could not afford to pay for a portrait of himself. The republican Ernie O'Malley writes of a rather later period that 'gentility flourished easily in Ireland; very little wealth nourished it'.[21] But they made up in cultural capital for what they lacked in ready cash, and compensated for genteel poverty with personal style. To value cultural over financial capital helped to mark them off from a vulgar commercial bourgeoisie, just as this, rather than conspicuous wealth, was what distinguished them from the common people. Taken together, they constituted a formidable intellectual power-house, which included one of the mathematical giants of the modern age (Hamilton), a world-famous medical school, a renowned political economist (Cairnes), one of Europe's finest palaeologists (Petrie), a chemist of international repute (Robert Kane) and one of the nineteenth century's most illustrious historians (Lecky). If they were not literally noblemen, they could aspire to a spiritual aristocratism; and this came to matter more as the economic and political gap between them and an aspiring Catholic middle class began to narrow. In a sense, they were a cross between a native and a colonial middle class, at home in Ireland as their counterparts in India were not, but still separated from the masses. Ideologically, they were caught between a species of colonial paternalism and a more native nationalism. Unlike the British ruling class, they were divided from the common people by religion and ethnicity, for which patriotism had to compensate.

They also resorted to that customary Irish alternative to material wealth, verbal opulence. It was an intensely oral culture, as well as an egregiously witty one. Some saw this as a mere off-shoot of Irish life as a whole: 'From every manor house and cabin ascends the incense of pleasant talk', rhapsodizes John B. Yeats in his *Essays Irish and American*.[22] The Rev. J. A. Galbraith, a Trinity mathematician, was said to be a mob orator of considerable talent. Lady Ferguson described social intercourse in Dublin as 'very agreeable', her favourite epithet along with 'refined', 'gracious' and 'delightful'. 'Receptions, dinners, balls, and concerts', she writes, 'promote gaiety and circulate money, and are gratifying to the populace, lessening the drain of absenteeism, which so seriously impairs the prosperity of Ireland'.[23] There was, in other words, a little bit for everyone: gaiety for the gentry, money for the middle classes and gratification for the masses, for whom the row of coaches at the Vice-Regal lodge was a consoling sign that money was being kept in the country, even if not much of it came their way. Lady Ferguson was not always so tender to the folk: elsewhere, she speaks disgustedly of the extension of the franchise from 'the trained, educated, and propertied classes, to the inexperienced and ignorant masses, who contribute little or nothing towards the burdens of the State'.[24]

John Pentland Mahaffy observed that he hailed from a country 'where the average man is able to talk well',[25] and ostentatiously dedicated his *Principles of the Art of Conversation*, in capital letters, to the Marchioness of Londonderry and Lady Aubrey Butler, 'being agreeable in conversation . . . the social result of Western civilisation'. Mahaffy saw conversation as an expression of 'that social instinct which is one of the strongest and best features of human nature',[26] and in the typical style of the Irish intellectual regarded general rather than specialized knowledge as more suitable to the art. He admired quickness of mind, and saw it as a distinctive quality of women. A culture which values wit over professional erudition is thus hospitable to women, since, as with Lady Morgan and Lady Wilde, it is an 'amateur' field in which those without higher education may shine. Mahaffy speaks up for the value of gossip, which is tantamount to speaking up for the value of Anglo-Irish Dublin, and notes with calculated litotes that in Ireland 'wit is less uncommon than elsewhere'.[27] He himself was a prime illustration of his own claim, observing as he did that the only character in the New Testament who asked for a drink of water was in hell. Asked if he was a clergyman, he responded, 'Yes, but not in any offensive sense of the term'. He also recalled that he was whipped only once as a child, for telling the truth. When he was suspended from preaching in Trinity for his heterodox theological views, Robert Tyrrell complained that he now suffered from insomnia in the college chapel.

As a clergyman, Mahaffy was really a thinly disguised pagan who could not forgive St Paul for not having attended the university of Antioch. He was a snobbish, conceited reactionary pathetically bedazzled by high society: 'Nothing but Lords in the house except for myself', he gleefully observed of a shooting party. On hearing the word Belfast, he is said to have inquired, 'Where is that near?' The only one of his slim volumes which reminds us that he is a cleric is *The Decay of Modern Preaching* (1882), which, conveniently enough for its author, argues that intelligence rather than piety is the prerequisite of an effective preacher, and stoutly defends the art of rhetoric. The most apparently extemporaneous flights of oratory, so he considers, result from careful calculation (a view shared by Richard Brinsley Sheridan), and Mahaffy is impatient with the notion that rhetoric is artificial and the non-rhetorical is natural. It is the voice of art, not nature, which speaks simply from the heart. His persuasive powers were thus clearly effective with at least one of his pupils, Oscar Wilde.

Mahaffy, described by Oliver St John Gogarty as 'the finest talker in Europe', saw contemporary Dublin as ancient Greece. Greek banquets, he wrote, 'were on the whole about as orderly as our gentlemen's parties, and intellectually something like an agreeable assemblage of university men, particularly among lively people like the Irish'.[28] Social sympathies he viewed as distinctively non-Anglo-Saxon: 'There is no people more distant and reserved in social intercourse [than the Anglo-Saxons], or that more resents any display of feeling, most of all sympathy'.[29] Despite his shameless toadying on the nobility (he had moved as a child from hobnobbing with German princes to the rather less patrician terrain of County Monaghan), and his lordly contempt for the Irish language ('sometimes useful to a man fishing for salmon or shooting grouse in the West'), he sent a donation to the nascent Abbey Theatre, supported his friend Lady Gregory in the Hugh Lane affair and unfavourably contrasted the soil of Attica with the 'Golden Vale of Tipperary'. Though unabashedly racist when it came to Celts – the Firbolgs, not they, had created ancient Irish art – he praised some aspects of popular Irish culture, criticized the landlords and the British administration in the country, and as the son of a Gaelic father felt generally superior to the boorish British. 'Just look at the Irish gob on him', a colleague irreverently remarked. Seeing himself as 'Irish of the Irish', he never wished to leave the country, unlike Anglo-Irish scholars like the historian J. B. Bury, and though he notoriously banned 'a man called Pearse' from addressing the Trinity students, he described himself as 'one of those splendid mongrels by whom the pure Irish have always been led'.[30] He never in fact led anyone, but could no doubt be allowed his harmless fantasy.

Wit, one might claim, is a socialized form of intellect, knowledge transmuted into style, manners, entertainment, and so appropriate to a caste whose ideas sprang more from the dinner table than the lecture theatre. Mahaffy described wit as 'a kind of social religion' whose rules ironically required spontaneity: it was not done to rehearse one's anecdotes. The Wildean or Shavian epigram typically inverts a piece of conventional English wisdom, as the Irish intellect comes to live negatively and parasitically off the reach-me-down truths of its colonial proprietors. The Victorian Anglo-Irish were heirs to a word-play, fantasy and verbal panache which can be found not only in the island's traditional literature, but also in Wolfe Tone's relish for what he called 'those strained quotations, absurd phrases and extravagant sallies which people in the unreserve of affectionate intercourse indulge themselves'.[31] Charles Lever, a word-spinner and '*bon raconteur* second only to Sheridan', as his friend William Wilde remarked of him, was a walking stereotype of the Anglo-Irish intellectual, dashing, boisterous, much given to mimicry and japery, full of crude animal spirits yet able to combine his unbuttoned *bonhomie* with the strenuous work of a provincial doctor. He did sterling work in this role during outbreaks of cholera in Derry and Portstewart, and like many of his Anglo-Irish *confrères* was a curious compound of high jinks and moral conscience.

49

Anglo-Irish gregariousness, however, blended oddly with an iso-
lating eccentricity. If they were a companionable crowd, quite a few
of them were also withdrawn, *dégagé*, spiritually or literally reclu-
sive. Antiquarian pursuits could straddle the divide, at once smell-
ing of the solitary scholar's lamp and part of a contentious public
sphere. But their political instability was echoed in a certain mental
precariousness, and the Anglo-Irish *esprit de corps* could be tinged
with a disturbing weirdness. Edward Stephens in his *My Uncle John*
describes the group as clinging together like members of a secret
society, and the mixture of the sociable and the esoteric is instructive. The poet William Allingham, marooned in the tedious provincial fastness of Ballyshannon, without literary colleagues or
intellectual conversation, complains bitterly of his boredom;[32] but
though the literary Dublin of the day indeed forms a contrast, it had
its share of hermits and grotesques. It was, comments W. J. Mc
Cormack, 'a town known for eccentricity rather than genius'.[33] This
was a trace of the aristocratic lifestyle, blending oddly with the more
pragmatic, hard-headed side of these worldly-wise bourgeois. (As
far as practicality goes, the physician Robert James Graves is re-
puted to have saved a ship from sinking in a storm by repairing the
pump with parts of his footwear.) If the practical Anglo-Irish poked
around in slums, they also moved in an alarmingly hermetic world.
Sheridan Le Fanu, who was both newspaper proprietor and Gothic
fantasist, locked himself away, Charles Maturin had to be forbidden
by his bishop from ceaseless frenetic dancing, while Archbishop
Whately, renowned as an irrepressible talker, could occasionally be
spotted swinging on chains in front of his episcopal palace smoking
a clay pipe.[34] The novelist Emily Lawless ended up as an eccentric
recluse in the Home Counties, while William Rowan Hamilton would
become violent when drunk. Mahaffy once crawled into a roomful
of clergymen dressed in a tigerskin rug. For all his cordiality, Charles
Lever had a brooding streak and was more or less hounded out of
Ireland to a more agreeably cosmopolitan life as author, diplomat
and traveller in Europe.

If the metropolitan Anglo-Irish were affable, exuberant and loquacious, they could also be profligate, capricious, spook-ridden,
fearfully superstitious, extravagantly self-destructive and idiosyn-

cratic to the point of incipient insanity. As a cross between burgher and bohemian, they displayed from time to time the anarchic life-style of those confidently in command. The hard-drinking, thriftless Isaac Butt, hardly a paragon of virtue himself, prosecuted his friend William Wilde for sexual assaulting his maid-servant. Like many a governing group, they tended to see themselves as personally dispensed from the social conventions of which they were the custodians. Weighty and reputable in themselves, they nevertheless preserved a secret pact with the vagrant, the deviant, the horror lurking in the attic. Protestant Gothic allows us a glimpse of this shadowy subtext or political unconscious, a world of decay, madness, loathing, solitude, lethal conflicts and paranoid insecurity, paralysed by the guilty burden of a blood-stained past which weighs like a nightmare on the brains of the living. It is a sense of treading on fearfully thin ice which was later to emerge in the novels of Elizabeth Bowen. J. M. Synge, who felt at once intimately at home on the Aran islands and profoundly estranged from their people, reverts constantly to the theme of the vagabond, pariah or internal exile.[35] If the Anglo-Irish moved at the hub of one civilization, they also felt themselves outcasts from another, and this ambivalence comes through in their peculiar mixture of buoyancy and precariousness. Owen Dudley Edwards sees them as a supremely self-confident coterie who thought themselves answerable to no one;[36] but while this captures one dimension of their minds, it neglects the extent to which they felt hunted and beleaguered. If they esteemed themselves highly, it was not necessarily because of a sanguine view of their future. The political anxiety which led them to criticize the Gaelic masses also drove them to set up home with them, as the traditional intellectual struggled to become an organic one.

Synge tries to resolve this ambiguity by identifying less with the common people as a whole than with a particular deviant or displaced wing of them. This reflects something of his own sidelined position within the Ascendancy, while allowing him to preserve something of their negative, sceptical attitude to the people as a whole. It is an ambiguity expressed in the Hiberno-English idiom of his drama, which appropriates an opulent English language for the common people while estranging them through their idiosyncratic use of it.[37] If the enlightened Anglo-Irish were outsiders struggling to get in, Sean O'Casey was an insider trying to get out – an organic intellectual of the urban working class who because of his inside knowledge had a patrician contempt for some of the culture he knew at first hand. Precisely because self-taught intellectuals like himself are homeless within their own class, they can castigate and speak up for it simultaneously. O'Casey's spiritual elitism is that of the insider who knows the common people all too well, and so is at once more and less at home with them than the liberal-minded Lady Gregorys. To be too much on the inside is to see the disconsolate, unvarnished truth which the populist Anglo-Irish intelligentsia idealize away, and thus in the end to retreat into a literal exile which outstrips in its critical distance the social *hauteur* of the Ascendancy. The neglected Revivalist wit and satirist Susan Mitchell comments perceptively of George Moore's vitriolic *Parnell and His Island* that the book 'is too bitter to be the work of an alien . . . a mere English settler would have felt none of the pain that shrieks from every page of [it]'.[38] As far as the literal exile of the erstwhile insider goes, James Joyce is a similar case in point – though Joyce was that rarest of combinations, an avant-gardist who was also a full-blooded democrat, at once more boldly experimental and more fascinated by the commonplace urban world than the Revivalists. The Yeats, Synges and Gregories, by contrast, stay geographically speaking at home and try to integrate.

At work here is what Raymond Williams has called a form of 'negative identification': the displaced patrician's tendency to make common cause with the people as a metaphor for his or her own aberrant status.[39] What appears like a tenderness to others is thus a kind of tenderness to oneself. You can find in the insecure state of the masses a reflection of your own marginality, either as a second-class ruling class in Ireland squeezed between Westminster and Daniel O'Connell, or as the artistic offspring of a philistine middle class. Synge often finds an echo of his own loneliness in what he sees as the solitude of the people as a whole. And the bearing of this condition on Yeats is equally evident. Like Oscar Wilde, Yeats was both cursed and privileged enough to be the child of a bohemian home, which deprived both men of a suitably demure object for their Oedipal revolt. But even in the homes of the non-artistic, culture was bound to bulk large in a group which defined itself so much in ethnic and religious terms, as the English bourgeoisie of the day had less need to do. Those in the grip of an identity crisis are likely to resort to history and culture, whereas the self-satisfied industrial middle classes of England were more fortunate in this respect.

The power of Anglo-Irish Dublin lay less in manufacture, though there was a strong commercial stratum, than in politics, scholarship, civic service, the learned professions and general social know-how. Socially remote from the agrarian issues with which some of them were preoccupied, they were forced into being a political class by such issues as the fate of the established church. A good many of them were clerics; but that most 'traditional' of all intellectual vocations, in Gramsci's eyes, was now at the eye of the political storm, plunged into the kind of ideological turbulence which traditional intellectuals can usually hope to escape. If the English country parsonage was a haven from political strife, the Irish one was at the vortex of the tithe war, the disestablishment question, the abolition of bishoprics and a range of other fiercely controversial political questions. The Irish established church was in turmoil less because of fossils and monkeys than because of the Whigs.

The Victorian Anglo-Irish were in W. J. Mc Cormack's terms 'an intricate if limited social group, less grand than they may have thought, but nevertheless powerful in business, in the professions, in education, in precisely those activities which defined Victorianism'.[40] There was a tight elite of them around the Vice-Regal lodge, which then spread out into a broader professional base. They were not for the most part professional writers, and not, like Bloomsbury or the Behan–Kavanagh–O'Brien clique, a literary coterie. 'Culture' meant for them something more social and substantial than *belles lettres*, and though they formed an intellectual circle, this, unlike Bloomsbury, was firmly rooted in their material and political power. Their home was the salon or scholarly institution rather than the artist's studio or louche cafe. Endangered by the tithe war, the Reform Bill, municipal reform, Whig reforms in church and state, the suppression of the Orange Order and the like, they were a

53

breeding ground for extreme Protestant supremacists (the young Le Fanu was a fanatical Tory) in a way notably at odds with the serenely Hellenic self-assurance that was one of their other personas. A governing bloc with its political back to the wall is likely to react rather more hysterically than those accustomed enough to being victimized, given the contrast with their previous condition; and the Dublin Ascendancy came to manifest as much rage, bewilderment and furious resentment as genial self-command. Well schooled in the cult of personality, they gave vent to their political high dudgeon by focusing it with admirable economy on the single demonized figure of Daniel O'Connell, who – crafty, devious, belligerent, bombastic, theatrical and falsely affable though he was, yet insolent enough to turn these despicable qualities to stunning political effect – represented everything they found most odious in the Gael. They betrayed the mixture of arrogance and disorientation, dominance and marginality which was historically typical of their class, and which is re-echoed today in so much Ulster Unionism. To regard oneself as one of the few remaining bastions of civilization is both self-congratulating and alarming.

Something of this ambivalence can be traced in one of the Victorian Ascendancy's most magnificent manifestos, Samuel Ferguson's celebrated *cri de coeur* on behalf of Protestant Ireland:

> Here are we, I say, who are the controllers of popery; the safeguards of British connection; the guarantees of the empire's integrity; the most respectable body of men for our members, in all Europe, whether we be considered with regard to wealth, industry, intellect, position, or absolute power; here are we, I say again, who in a word, are the arbiters of Britain's fate, deceived, insulted, spoiled, and set at defiance. . . . Deserted by the Tories, insulted by the Whigs, threatened by the Radicals, hated by the Papists, and envied by the Dissenters, plundered in our country-seats, robbed in our town houses, driven abroad by violence, called back by humanity, and, after all, told that we are neither English nor Irish, fish nor flesh, but a peddling colony, a forlorn advanced guard that must conform to every mutinous movement of the proletarian rabble.[41]

If Ferguson's feelings are raw and dishevelled, his style effortlessly transcends them in its poise and *gravitas*. The buoyancy of his rhetoric, with its measured parataxis and antitheses, its scrupulously disciplined indignation, gives the lie to the paranoid passion which drives the passage forward. 'Head' and 'Heart', which speak alternately in this tormented dialogue, come together in a contradictory unity of form and content. As often in Irish letters, it is the integrity and exuberance of language itself which offers an edge over the bleakness of its content.

········

It was in the *Dublin University Magazine* – 'the supreme archive of Irish Victorian experience', as W. J. McCormack has dubbed it[42] – that this embattled class found its corporate intellectual expression. Founded in 1833 as a spirited reaction to Catholic Emancipation, the Reform Bill, the tithe war and the threatened abolition of ten bishoprics, the *DUM* was the first successful monthly periodical in Ireland, and was to survive until 1877. By then, it had gone through twelve editors, ten proprietors and ten publishers. It thus spanned the generations from Maria Edgeworth to George Moore. Founded by six Trinity men, including Ferguson, Anster, Samuel Lover, Caesar Otway, Isaac Butt and its first editor Charles Stanford, it strove in the words of one commentator to 'beat back the forces of emancipation and democracy',[43] and in the style of its great mentor Edmund Burke to raise the gut instincts of the gentry to the dignity of a political philosophy. To this extent, it fitted Gramsci's notion of an organic intelligentsia, shaping and elaborating the inarticulate common sense of Protestant Ireland. Though if Gramsci's organic intellectuals are typically the spokespersons of an emergent group or class, the *DUM* was the voice of a dying one. It was in this sense an 'intellectual' rather than an 'academic' organ, organizing a sphere of public opinion, popularizing a creed and crystallizing new forms of Anglo-Irish identity. If Trinity provided it with its intellectual muscle, it was nevertheless formally independent of the college.

Isaac Butt wrote that the journal had 'more popular, and far more important objects . . . to send forth to the world [than] a chronicle of scientific intelligence, or a register of academic proceedings'.[44] He himself, as a prototypical intellectual, contributed essays in a range

55

of genres: fiction, politics, law, economics. Despite its organic function, a high proportion of its moving spirits were those most exemplary of traditional intellectuals, clergymen; and this comes near to capturing the contradictoriness of the enterprise as a whole. The magazine, rather like Young England, was a vibrant defence of conservatism, promoting a reformed version of the status quo with the kind of youthful vigour and *élan* one would more readily associate with the Young Turks of a progressive newspaper. One decade later, the *Nation* was to promote a rather different blending of radicalism and conservatism. In the hands of the *DUM* literati, as in those of a Disraeli, a backward-looking or mildly reformist politics became a matter of imaginative flair and vision, delivered with all the dynamism of the iconoclast.[45] Only thus, no doubt, would the squires of the shires be shaken from their dogmatic slumber. The elite, simply to survive, had now to become an avant-garde. An elevated, comprehensive view of Irish culture had become a militant position.

Before the *DUM*, periodicals in Ireland had on the whole fared badly. It was a society either too poor to buy them or too politically fissured to provide any one of them with a large enough readership. The Anglo-Irish rather snobbishly took in leading London journals like *Fraser's*, *Blackwood's* and *The Gentleman's Magazine*, when their colonial apathy moved them to read at all. The *DUM* thus broke the mould, openly modelling itself on *Fraser's* and *Blackwood's* in what one critic sees as 'their heavy humour, their rudeness and reactionary fanaticism',[46] but unmistakably Irish, not least in its embattled Orange tone.[47] Charles Gavan Duffy thought the journal more libellous of the Irish people than the London *Times*.[48] There was a good deal of adolescent facetiousness and laboured verbosity, in the manner of precocious young intellectuals.[49] With Charles Lever at the editorial helm the magazine became more urbane, breezier in tone and broader in appeal; its sales accordingly soared. The affable, middle-brow Lever lowered the tone and expanded the literary side of the journal, infusing it with something of the eirenic good humour of his fiction, which he published there in plenty. William Carleton also published several of his novels in its pages, and Charles Maturin was on its staff. It became less 'national' under some later editors, losing some of its readers, but when Sheridan Le Fanu took up the editorial chair, national topics were resumed and its circulation was restored. Declining throughout the 1850s, it survived long enough to witness a few contributions from Oscar Wilde. For all its rancour and special pleading, it was an enterprise of rare quality and tenacity, ranking among the finest literary achievements of nineteenth-century Ireland. J. C. Beckett sees it as encouraging a serious literary representation of Ireland, and Thomas Davis, who never wrote for it, praised it as having alone maintained the reputation of Irish genius.[50] In the Introduction to the 1852 edition of his *Traits and Stories of the Irish Peasantry*, William Carleton calls the periodical 'a bond of union for literary men of every class . . . a neutral spot in a country where party feeling runs so high, on which the Roman Catholic priest and the Protestant parson, the Whig, the Tory, and the radical, divested of their respective prejudices, can meet in an amicable spirit'. It is a familiar Arnoldian note in nineteenth-century Ireland: culture as the imaginary reconciliation of real conflicts, and this claimed of a journal renowned for its contempt for popular democracy.

The brothers Samuel and Mortimer O'Sullivan, Gaelic Catholics who became Protestant conservatives, were the moving spirits behind much of the early magazine, with Samuel as perhaps its leading ideologue. A taste of their politics may be had in Mortimer O'Sullivan's *Letter to Daniel O'Connell*, which claims that Protestants have grievances too, excuses oppressive political measures as an essential response to popular discontent and accuses O'Connell of intimidation. With uncharacteristic reticence, O'Sullivan refuses to enter into argument about Catholic Emancipation, or about how blameworthy the British in Ireland have been. O'Connell is frightening capital away from Ireland and disaffecting Catholics who have no just cause for complaint.[51] The magazine always had this vein of redneckery, not least in its early years, but it was one at odds with its exalted 'national' spirit, as well as with much of its finest writing. If it feared the common people, it also courted their cause with the best kind of *noblesse oblige*; if it could betray the giddiness and flippancy of its more scurrilous English counterparts, it also had the *gravitas*, intellectual seriousness and moral conscience of the Victorian sages.

As with all Ascendancy attempts at spiritual and political leadership, the *DUM* was self-serving and self-sacrificial at the same time. It was a heroic phase of a historically doomed project, which sought, impossibly, to refurbish a ruling class on the brink of being accused of genocide by placing it in the van of a national cultural revival. The Irish Revival was to fail in its turn in just the same venture. 'Who leads revolution in other countries?', the poet Aubrey de Vere asked William Smith O'Brien in private correspondence, replying to his own rhetorical query, 'the nobles'. But in Ireland, he gloomily adds, the nobles are 'despised abroad and hated at home'.[52] In any case, how could 'culture' unite the nation, when in its narrow aesthetic sense it meant works from which the common people were excluded, and in its broader anthropological sense signified the very issues – religion, custom, identity, ethnicity – on which the nation was most divided? It was not, to be sure, by culture alone that the Anglo-Irish intelligentsia hoped to redeem the times, despite Samuel Ferguson's forlorn comment that 'we must fight our battles now with a handful of types and a composing-stick'.[53] The journal was full of hard-nosed political and economic analysis, and pressed its programmatic demands on a whole range of quotidian questions. The writings of Isaac Butt, one of Ireland's greatest, least sung conservative champions of popular reform, are exemplary here. But it was still hard to square the circle between a disinterested plan for national salvation and the sectoral political interests of those who promoted it.

....

Something of this contradiction can be seen at its most spectacular in the writings of Jane Elgee (Lady Wilde), a veritable *pot pourri* of nationalist sentiment and Anglo-Irish condescension. In her rhapsodically written *Social Studies*, she sketches a militantly feminist history of the human race, which concludes in typically cavalier fashion by announcing that 'we have now traced the history of women from Paradise to the nineteenth century'.[54] If her political zest is admirable, her scholarship leaves a little to be desired. Yet her feminism is coolly interwoven with the racism of her class: 'the flat-faced, square-headed, small-eyed Calmuch, a mean and sinister-looking people, yet with intellect enough to hold women in bondage', have little to be said for them, while Eskimos are half fish and half human. Elgee proposes a scheme for female lectureships and professorships, though she also considers, strangely in the light of her less than angelic husband, that women have a natural tendency to gaze on men of genius as gods. She looks with sympathy on Chinese female infanticide, thinks Henry VIII did 'too little' in executing his wives and remarks that any woman would give her head to be crowned queen for a day, an oddly contradictory claim. Though she scorned Home Rule from a vaguely separatist standpoint, she also hobnobbed with the Lord Lieutenant. If she is non-conformist ('the best chance, perhaps, of domestic felicity is when all the family are Bohemian'),[55] she also holds that the muscles of the female mouth should be trained to achieve beauty. The book praises wit and epigram and mourns the death of individuality, but speaks in doing so of 'insignificant people'. Literary women require cool and light dress: 'No stiff corselet should depress the full impulses of a passionate heart',[56] and wearing black should be avoided as it absorbs light and spoils the effect of rooms.

Full of praise for British imperialism ('that wonderful and indomitable English enterprise which pervades the world'),[57] Elgee emerges as a full-blooded triumphalist on the question of progress and enlightenment, a doctrine which then instantly collides with her nationalism. Ireland, with its millions of lost people, 'without commerce, without literature, without a flag, without dignity – in a word, without self-government',[58] is a wretched exception to this universal trend. But almost all its problems could be resolved by shipping its inhabitants out to Australia, 'but a pleasure trip of 40 days'. There is no strife in the Antipodes, since the aboriginals are almost extinct, and two million Irish might emigrate there with profit, along with three million Londoners thrown in for good measure. Elgee seems not to have noticed that some of her compatriots are already being busily shipped to the Antipodes, not least a few of her erstwhile colleagues in Young Ireland, though it is doubtful that these convicted felons found the trip quite as pleasurable as she imagines.

Elgee was in her day a genuinely courageous militant, and a robust campaigner for women's rights. Her name headed a list of 10,000 women's signatures on a petition presented to Trinity College in 1892 demanding the admission of women. She also had some impressive intellectual credentials,[59] including in her *Notes on Men, Women, and Books* what must be one of the only nineteenth-century Irish essays on the German philosopher Jean-Paul Richter. But the natural insouciance of the aristocrat is hard to distinguish from the iconoclasm of the rebel. If she speaks up for her sex, she also disparages them: 'no woman is really learned', and their charm lies in their 'light superficiality'. The 'unsufferably prosy' George Eliot, full of 'pretentious commonplace', writes in *Middlemarch* of petty people in a petty town. An essay on O'Connell highlights his hostility to republicanism and his 'courteous' submission to authority, along with the 'excessive beauty and whiteness' of his forehead. The common Irish are false, cruel and malignant as well as free, open and generous, unfit for a republic. Yet in her work on ancient Irish legends she believes the Irish ('simple, joyous, reverent, and unlettered')[60] to be privy to a 'primal creed and language of humanity', an esoteric truth descended from the early Iranians and Egyptians and preserved from the masses by the priests. Irish mythology, in short, is the archetypal unconscious of the human race, and the genial, laughter-loving nature of the Irish themselves is best expressed in the elves.

In her travel book *Driftwood from Scandanavia*, which describes reindeer as tasting like sliced boot, Elgee opposes the abolition of the Irish landlords: 'how will the condition of the nation be advanced by the robbing of one class to feed another? One shudders to think of Ireland mapped out into five million potato plots, each fenced by its rude stone wall; the beautiful and the picturesque utterly sacrificed without even wealth being gained, for all progress will be rendered impossible. Progress requires capital and culture, science and knowledge',[61] and without its landowners Ireland will revert to primeval bog. Tenant proprietorship is thus rejected among other things on aesthetic grounds. All this, to be sure, is the later, post-revolutionary Elgee, a far cry from her incendiary verses for the *Nation*. She is writing in the wake of a failed insurrection, when the unpalatable petty-bourgeois Fenians have seized the revolutionary initiative from the genteel souls of Young Ireland. But the ideological ambivalences of the upper-class radical persist throughout her exotic career, as a patrician preoccupation with style, bravura and romance can veer either to left or right. As with Yeats, the nonchalance of the nobility finds an echo in the anarchic streak of the underdog, thus by-passing the aesthetically unappetizing middle classes. But if this anti-bourgeois iconoclasm is radical in respect of the hot-faced money-changers, it also contemns the nationalist middle class which was to do rather more for Irish underdogs than write poetry about them. Lady Gregory writes in *Ideals in Ireland* that her object was to reveal the movement of Irish thought to those who 'look beyond politics and horses',[62] a phrase which betrays the link between the aristocrat's distaste for philistinism and her aversion to the political practice which might do something about it.

From the *DUM* and the *Nation* to Yeats and the Literary Revival, the most typical ideology of the Romantic nationalist is radical conservatism. If it is populist, compassionate, anti-commercial and anti-utilitarian, it is also elitist, paternalist, backward-looking and anti-political. It is the doctrine of most of those from Coleridge to Ruskin who make up Raymond Williams's 'Culture and Society' lineage, and an Irishman, Edmund Burke, stands at the fountainhead of both traditions. It is also the *credo* of a good many European modernists. In Ireland, however, it has a specifically female dimension. Style, personality, social compassion, a sympathy for the rebel, a distaste for ruling powers and orthodoxies, a remoteness from politics and commerce: it is not hard to see why this should be the peculiar province of educated yet disadvantaged women. Lady Morgan stands squarely in this current, as does Lady Augusta Gregory a century later.[63] Again and again, women in Ireland provide the 'spiritual' or poetic dimension of a nationalism too mesmerized by immediate political struggle to reflect on its deeper resources. The male aristocrat, or (as with Yeats) pseudo-aristocrat, acts as a counterpart to these women, converting his distance from workaday middle-class matters into an opportunity to raise more searching philosophical questions.[64] Constance Markiewicz and Maud Gonne inherit the flamboyance, elitism and radical impulse of this heritage, though with them, in what is now a revolutionary epoch, it has become intensively politicized.

A rather less extravagant version of Jane Elgee's ideological conflicts can be found in the work of a fellow woman writer, Emily
Lawless. Daughter of the third baron Cloncurry, whose father was
embroiled in the United Irish insurrection, Catholic Emancipation
and the anti-tithe campaign, Lawless sprang from an impeccably
liberal-Ascendancy lineage, a nationally minded sympathizer with
land reform who none the less retained close links with the British
political establishment in Ireland. Her well executed history of Ireland is reasonably even-handed: critical of the United Irishmen, but
sensitive to government atrocities against them, she is as generous
as she can manage to O'Connell, while upbraiding him for having
snapped the people's ties of feudal fealty to their landlords.
Cromwell's military violence is somewhat excused, though not his
plantations, and while Thomas Davis is to be admired, Fintan Lalor
is a monomaniac.[65] Her equally stylish historical novel, *With Essex in
Ireland* (1890), with its deft handling of military action and restrained imitation of Elizabethan English, finds its prototypically
unreliable narrator in the Earl of Essex's secretary, who shies from
English brutality in Ireland yet is full of stereotyped prejudices about
the need to treat the natives roughly. Though Lawless is stronger on
description than narrative, she could write even more finely about
the natives than she could of their rulers. *Grania* (1892), a tale set
among a starved Aran fishing community, is slow-moving but splen-
didly atmospheric, revealing an acute ear for idiom and gossip as
well as a streak of early feminism. The rebellious, fiercely independent Grania, daughter of a fisherman, struggles against being en-
snared in wedlock to her drunken lover and dies a solitary heroic
death. Lawless's fictional masterpiece, however, is *Hurrish* (1886), a
bleak tragedy of the Burren poor which brought its author into a
lengthy correspondence with Gladstone.

An essay by Lawless on the Famine, which accuses the British
government of running a botched relief operation, reveals a re-
sourceful sympathy with the common people.[66] But the melancholic decline and fall of the gentry is also an abiding motif, as the
story 'O'Donnell's Report' tells the tale of an old servant's loyalty to
a courageous landlord under threat of assassination.[67] Lawless's
excellent biography of Maria Edgeworth, which consciously sets

62

out to rescue her as an Irish novelist from the English critics, is a witty, ironic, irreverent treatment of its subject, not least of the 'patriarchal' Richard Edgeworth's penchant for arranging suitably compliant females like satellites around him. Edgeworth, she acidly remarks, elevated Maria's worst fault, lack of imagination, into a kind of 'solemn duty', so that her lack of it swelled and grew under his fosterage. He was, she comments, a man who never got drunk even when politeness might have required it. Maria's letters she regards as the finest ever written by an 'Englishwoman', though her Irish novels suffer from a certain falsity consequent on her childhood absence from the country. Judiciously even-handed on the 1798 rebellion, though darkly suspecting that it was incited by the British government, she is suitably sardonic about Maria's sanguineness in the midst of military terror, more concerned with her cats than with the massacres raging around her. *Castle Rackrent*, from which moral concerns are 'startlingly absent', is seen as a subversive text, which Lawless imaginatively compares with the amoralism of Defoe. It is a novel which seems to 'stand outside of the entire code, human or divine . . . wholly independent and revolutionary', free, unlike some of Edgeworth's later Irish fiction (though she lavishes some high praise on *The Absentee*), of any too schematic ideological purpose. Ireland, she considers, has claimed too little place in the nation's literature, a default which her own impressive fiction does something to repair. Yet Lawless's imaginative sympathies were finally overtaken by the political prejudices she inherited from her class, as she retreated in her last years, disenchanted with the Home Rule controversy, to a secluded life in Surrey.

A similar tension marks the work of one of nineteenth-century Ireland's most archetypal traditional intellectuals, the Catholic poet, landowner and Newmanite Aubrey de Vere. Offspring of the Limerick nobility, de Vere was a discipline of Burke and Kant, an enemy of Benthamite, materialist, empiricist and radical thought who was influenced by F. D. Maurice, briefly associated with the Cambridge Apostles and came to know both Wordsworth and Tennyson. Converting to Catholicism, he retired to his estate and produced such abysmal verse as 'Ireland in the Olden Time', a lamentable verse-record of historic national events which artfully avoids the present and recent past in its remorselessly churchy, chivalric high-mindedness. De Vere, who became professor of literature at Newman's university, was an ultramontane reactionary who detested democracy, decried the Fenians and regretted the irreligious communism of the lower classes. As a young man, however, he produced one of the finest, much neglected 'national' texts of the period, *English Misrule and Irish Misdeeds*, which alarmed some of his fashionable English friends by its ardour for reform. It is a dignified, eloquent defence of the Irish against the calumnies of the English, a habit he warns may be perilous: 'My countrymen have many peculiarities, and amongst others this one, that the more you revile them, the less they like you'.[68] The bathos is handled with lethal dexterity. The *gravitas*, sardonic wit and icily controlled indignation of the book are highly impressive, as de Vere ritually turns English slanders of the Irish back on themselves. If the Irish have their blarney, the English have that rather less innocuous form of falsehood known as cant. 'You who attribute to the Irish peasant a want of truth, why did you render it impossible for the Irish peasant to answer plainly a simple question, "Where does your priest live?"'[69] If the English accuse the Irish of procrastination, what else characterized their own handling of Catholic Emancipation? ('You were not so slow', de Vere remarks, 'in your conquest of India'.) Irish pauperism is indeed to be lamented, but 'that a vast and growing pauperism should exist in the heart of infinite wealth' in Britain is even more to be mourned. There is a direct connection, he points out, 'between the wealth of your nation and the poverty of the obscure millions who produce that wealth'.[70] These are more the sentiments of John Mitchel than John Henry Newman.

The later de Vere, however, was rather less of a cheer leader for the plain people of Ireland. His *Recollections* sneers at the Chartists and opposes the enfranchising of 'ignorant cottiers'.[71] An essay of 1887 advocates the repression of agrarian agitators, the rejection of Home Rule and a form of proportional representation which will ensure the pre-eminence in parliament of the wise, propertied, intellectual classes. Peasant proprietorship may help to stem revolution, though the state, which cannot 'govern through love', has a duty to oppose dissent with coercion. Partisan Ireland has lacked a moderate, civilizing public opinion, though de Vere's own views are neither moderate nor particularly civilized. In an intemperate tirade against naturalism, modernity, materialism and decadent sensualism, he sanctimoniously commends Ferguson's poetry as a paragon of a wholesome, non-sceptical, unmorbid art, as well as putting in a word for the 'timeless' achievement of Coventry Patmore's now deservedly derided poem 'The Angel in the House'.[72]

········

The great verse saga of embattled Anglo-Ireland is Samuel Ferguson's *Congal*, published in 1872 but begun some thirty years earlier. Its period of composition runs parallel to Tennyson's publication of his Arthurian *Idylls*, of which it is in some sense an Irish analogue. Both poets are aiming to produce national epics, in distinctly less propitious conditions than Spenser or Milton. The work is cast in an irritatingly jangling iambic metre which Ferguson nevertheless handles with admirable deftness, like a man playing subtly on a trombone. Like much of his verse, with the fine exception of his 'Lament for the Death of Thomas Davis', the poem lacks inwardness, as its landscapes of the mind are relentlessly externalized; and this externalization (Ferguson's lyric talent deserted him fairly early) may well reflect his need to speak out as a public poet in a condition of political crisis. It is just that poetry and the public sphere no longer amicably coexist, not least in a Victorian era when the novel has seized the role of social commentary. *Congal* is sturdily well-wrought verse, but too monotonously heroic in tone and restricted in sensibility, with a good many *longueurs*. Aubrey de Vere, evidently in masochistic mood, inquired of Ferguson's wife as to when her husband would give them another *Congal*. In his rollicking metres, as well as in his constricted emotional range and Victorian imperialist admiration for the more muscular virtues, Ferguson is the Irish Kipling. The poem is like some intricate piece of stoutly fashioned, rather rusty machinery washed up in the mid-nineteenth century from some earlier mode of production. Its central conflict is between Congal himself, king of Ulster and leader of the last pagan bards, and Domnal, Christian monarch of Ireland, a struggle in

65

which Congal is worsted and slain. It is not hard to decode this as a war between the free-spirited Protestant intellectuals and the repressive clerics, though the allegory is multiple. Since Congal is fighting for independence, his Ulster also perhaps represents Ireland as a whole against Britain. This then neatly blends Irish nationalism with Ulster supremacism.

Ferguson's anti-clericalism takes a somewhat less exalted form in his flat-footed, intensely unfunny anti-papist squib 'Father Tom and the Pope, or a Night in the Vatican', penned on the eve of Catholic Emancipation, in which the pretentious ignoramus Father Tom and the pope spend a night of blarneying, boozing and neo-scholastic quibbling together, all cast in an atrocious stage-Irish. Knockabout comedy was hardly the forte of this austerely honest Ulsterman. If the *DUM* as a whole has its mixture of the roguish and the high-flown, so does the work of Ferguson, who was one of its regular contributors.

Ferguson had an intriguing theory of Irish history, which he formulates in his celebrated *DUM* critique of James Hardiman's *Irish Minstrelsy* (1831).[73] For him, the histories of Ireland and Britain are out of synchrony, since Ireland, bound as it was through an excess of local pieties and tribal devotion to a pre-feudal clannishness, never underwent feudalism and an allegiance to a sovereign, which for Ferguson count as essential phases in the long trek to Protestant liberty. The two countries, one pre- and one post-feudalist, could thus never properly meet in the middle, as Britain had already travelled through these phases and left them behind. It is, in classical Marxist parlance, a problem of combined and uneven development: the two nations 'are still unable to amalgamate from the want of these intermediate steps upon the public scale – steps forgotten by the one and never taken by the other'. They are stranded on either side of an historical watershed, confronting one another across a well-nigh unspannable abyss. This contradiction fissures Ireland internally too, exhibiting as it does 'anomalous features of mixed crudeness and maturity'.

Translation, however – Ferguson's abiding political theme, as well as a significant slice of his poetic practice – may still be possible. What is needed is for the Irish 'clansman' to be borne forward into modernity, his myopic pieties redirected to monarch and society as a whole, while the modern English utilitarian must be simultaneously regressed to rediscover his bonds of affection with countryfolk. The Irish, in short, must be universalized into *Gesellschaft*, while the English must be re-rooted in *Gemeinschaft*, so that each nation may meet the other coming the other way.

Ferguson's own English versions of Irish poetry then provide a microcosm of this political fusion, as what cannot be pulled off in political reality can be achieved instead in language. By rendering the Gaelic text in an English at once civil and faithful, the political union of Britain and Ireland, or Anglo-Irish and Gael, can be re-enacted at the level of discourse. The English verbal form draws the uncouth Gaelic content into the universalizing sphere of modernity, while being itself rooted and replenished by the Gaelic poetry's more robust energies. It is a delicate balance to strike, as Ferguson rightly takes to task the bland, overbred English translations of Hardiman's volume, while elsewhere taking a decidedly condescending view of Carolan. He also praises Thomas Moore for having detached some enchanting Irish airs from 'their unworthy connection' with vulgar Irish words.[74] The Gaelic bard reappears in Ferguson as the Victorian sage, while the ancient Irish heroes are converted into aristocratic leaders in an age of mass Catholic democracy. Culture, once again, is the disinterested ground upon which all the Irish may converge – a notion which can itself be translated, as the historian Tom Dunne suggests, into 'the colonisation of Gaelic literature in the interests of the Anglo-Irish Ascendancy'.[75] As the bard of a 'national' rather than sectarian culture, Ferguson nevertheless believed that the ideal solution to Catholicism would be to wean its deluded devotees from it altogether. Dispirited and defeatist, the later Ferguson was to pen a couple of latently hysterical sub-Browningesque monologues about the Fenian murders in Phoenix Park. The Heart had finally triumphed over the Head.

....

If a single figure epitomizes the Anglo-Irish intelligentsia of the day, it is the historian William Edward Hartpole Lecky. One of Gramsci's

67

traditional intellectuals, Lecky was a gentleman scholar rather than a don, detached from popular movements and increasingly at odds with a democratic age. He was the scion of an aristocratic family and was himself an absentee landlord, a Whiggish apologist for the Protestant Patriot tradition of eighteenth-century Ireland and a fervent discipline of Henry Grattan. It was nationality rather than nationalism he championed, and as a liberal Unionist he regarded the Anglo-Irish elite as the custodians of this flame. His great study of European rationalism brought him the friendship of leading English writers, and as an Irish cosmopolitan he travelled often enough in Europe to be described as an 'absentee man of letters'. He was equally catholic in his intellectual interests, with the audaciously broad scope of the classical humanist; his books favour the synoptic view in the teeth of a growing professionalization of knowledge. Indeed, his interest in the *longues durées*, the great, slow-moving, persistent forces of modern civilization, reflects his deliberate remoteness from the arena of petty politics,[76] as well as a certain Positivist preference for the social over the political. The historian 'must study the slow process of growth as well as the moment of efflorescence, the long progress of decay as well as the final catastrophe'.[77] 'History is never more valuable', he writes, 'than when it enables us, standing as on a height, to look beyond the smoke and turmoil of our petty quarrels, and to detect in the slow developments of the past the great permanent forces that are steadily bearing nations onward to improvement or decay'.[78] It is the voice of the traditional intellectual, who finds in history the transcendent vantage-point which some of his Irish contemporaries are discovering in science or culture. In its scorn for the political sphere, this viewpoint ironically reflects a privileged position within it. Yet if this pursuit of the *longue durée* was in one sense a riposte to Irish political myopia, it also reflected a society in which political contentions had their roots in a long history, as well as in questions which went well beyond the narrowly political. Aubrey de Vere speaks of the formation of public opinion as 'a sort of crystallisation which must take place by a slow process, if the result is to be solid and definite in shape; and in Ireland the ardour of our political temperature produces too rapid a precipitation'.[79] It is remarkable how many Irish political thinkers, of both left and right, were allergic to politics.

Lecky was one of the last of the great non-academic historians, in a lineage stretching from Gibbon and Macaulay to Acton and Froude – a 'philosopher-historian'[80] who was also a popularizer, a man of public affairs and an associate of some of the weightier dignitaries of his age. Donal McCartney points out that he wrote at a point of transition in Europe from history to sociology, as Comte, Buckle, Dilthey and Herbert Spencer were coming to dominate the intellectual scene.[81] As a London clubman he placed himself at the centre of the social and intellectual life of the metropolis, launching interventions into Irish affairs from the Athenaeum. If he was an historian, he was also a sage, popular philosopher and intellectual leader. He also crossed the frontier between historian and *belletrist*, taking immense pains with his style despite being an execrable poet. Noted for his temperate, dignified rebuttal of J. A. Froude's rancorous *History of Ireland*,[82] his own politics waxed more rancorous and rearguard as Catholic nationalism rose steadily to power. He was elected Unionist MP for Dublin University, opposed Home Rule and tried to galvanize his fellow Unionists into action against nationalism and democracy. In fact he became the leading spokesman for conservative Unionism against Gladstone, whose turn to Irish affairs might ironically have been partly inspired by some of Lecky's earlier writings. Like several of his Anglo-Irish *confrères*, he ended up as an immoderate in the cause of moderation, a phenomenon not unknown in the Ireland of today.

It was not perhaps wholly by chance that nineteenth-century Ireland should have produced a great historian of ideas. 'Religious opinions', Lecky writes, 'grow out of different states of society, reflect their civilisation, and are altogether moulded and coloured by their modes of thought'.[83] If he was among other things a sociologist of ideas in a tradition from Vico and Herder to Comte and Buckle, it was partly because philosophical idealism was harder to sustain in a society where ideas were so palpably shaped by political interests. To live in Ireland was to be a spontaneous materialist: the political economist John Elliot Cairnes, a liberal Unionist rather than a Marxist, declares his belief in 'how extensively the material interests of men prevail in determining their political opinions and conduct'.[84] Prefiguring the philosophy of *fin-de-siècle* Europe, Lecky believed that changes in ideas and opinions were inspired by profound, by no means wholly rational historical processes – another doctrine not hard to credit in Ireland. 'In every age and society', he writes in his study of European rationalism, 'there operates a "hidden bias of the imagination"' which runs deeper than rational argument, and which – rather as with Michel Foucault's *episteme* – forms the matrix within which such rationality develops.[85] His historicism thus challenged rationalism in the philosophical meaning of the word, while his politics fought to maintain it in a looser sense. He also tried to salvage his ethical thought from the implicit relativism of the historicist view, an essential move if he was to combat his political opponents on firm moral ground. If politically turbulent societies breed a certain scepticism of ahistorical values, they also foster a certain need for them.

So it is that Lecky begins his great *History of European Morals* with a long, earnest refutation of utilitarianism in the name of a transcendent morality. The book, he remarks in its preface, is strongly opposed to a school of philosophy 'which is at present extremely influential in England'. Virtue he defines deontologically, as not necessarily conducive to happiness; it is duty, rather than pleasure or self-interest, which must reign supreme. Like Henry Fielding in *Tom Jones*, he holds that the doctrine that virtue will reap its reward in this world has only one flaw, namely that it is not true. Indeed, history shows that 'a career of consistent rapacity, ambition, selfishness, and fraud may be eminently conducive to national prosperity'.[86] Utilitarianism is in direct conflict with common language and common sentiments, and should be dismissed in favour of 'the supreme and transcendent excellence of moral good'.[87] Along with Anglo-Irish anti-empiricists like William Rowan Hamilton, he denies that moral values can be derived from experience and falls back instead on the intuitionist ethics of a Francis Hutcheson, positing a special moral faculty which is as immediate and self-evident as the aesthetic sense. When it comes to his moral duty, the Victorian gentleman just knows what he should do. He thus finds himself awkwardly caught between a sociologism of ideas and an absolutism of ethics, which is never satisfactorily resolved. Moral principles remain constant in themselves, but their application varies historically, as does the degree to which they are acted upon and the kind of virtues which an age will highlight. 'There is a certain sense in which moral distinctions are absolute and immutable', he writes. 'There is another sense in which they are altogether relative and transient'.[88] In a later work, he writes that 'while the primary and essential elements of right and wrong remain unchanged, nothing is more certain than that the standard or ideal of duty is constantly changing', so that 'a very humane man in another age may have done things which would now be regarded as atrociously barbarous'.[89] The implied definition of 'humane' is noteworthy: the concept is defined not by what one does, but by how one feels.

Lecky thus holds in Comtean fashion to a kind of natural history of morality, which evolves by definite stages. As with a modern moral philosopher like Alasdair MacIntyre, he recognizes that the virtues are bound up with different forms of social life.[90] But this view is at odds with his patrician refusal to reduce morals to the mere offspring of society, as his intellect takes him in one direction and his ideology in another. There is a similar tension in his attitude to historical progress, a notion which is implicit in his historicism but at odds with his conservative ethics. Progress does indeed take place – 'Gunpowder and military machinery have rendered the triumph of the barbarians impossible'[91] – but moral and material prosperity by no means go hand-in-hand. 'Had the Irish peasants been less chaste', he remarks, 'they would have been more prosperous', meaning no doubt that chastity would have forced them into fewer improvident marriages. Though humane sentiments have been historically on the increase, this moral gain has been at the cost of such virtues as heroism, loyalty, enthusiasm and the spirit of reverence. If Lecky's sociologism is impeccably progressivist, some of his moral values remain quasi-feudalist.

The book which was to win him European celebrity – his *History of the Rise and Influence of the Spirit of Rationalism in Europe* – reveals his more progressivist face. Lecky emerges here as what we might call today, after J. G. A. Pocock, a Whig commercial humanist, seeing the evolution of industry as fostering tolerance and civility, and the history of rationalism as culminating in liberty and peace.[92]

71

Its latest task is to divert the threat of socialism by disseminating the principles of political economy among the working classes. The book is a magnificent apologia for intellectual freedom, another doctrine which it is not surprising to see springing from clericist Ireland. With its vivid accounts of superstition, oppression, intolerance, persecution and sectarian hatred through the ages, it argues that there has been no greater moral force in human history than Christianity, and no bloodier institution than the Roman Catholic Church. A rationalist, disinterested defence of intellectual tolerance is thus ironically in Irish terms a polemical political position in itself. 'Ireland', he observes with barely concealed repugnance, 'is now the only civilised country where public opinion is governed, not occasionally but habitually, by theological considerations'.[93] The two fundamental tendencies of the human mind can be labelled rationalist and Roman Catholic, a dichotomy which is hardly an instance of dispassionate rationalism. In Newmanite fashion, Lecky praises the love of truth for its own sake, in short supply though it is: 'love of truth is not common in one sex, [and] is almost unknown in the other'.[94] This statement too is offered as the upshot of a disinterested love of truth. What Lecky applauds as impartiality is in fact the antitype of the organic, *engagé* Irish intellectual. 'Nothing can be more fatal in politics', he announces, 'than a preponderance of the philosophical, or in philosophy than a preponderance of the political spirit'.[95] It is an opinion quite at odds with the spirit of the *DUM*, which sought precisely to interfuse these pursuits. But Lecky's view that 'a disinterested love of truth can hardly coexist with a strong political spirit'[96] also captures some of that journal's inconsistencies. The Germans, he considers, are capable of high abstractions because of the languor of their politics, a point which Karl Marx made in slightly less patronizing style. In fact, Lecky's own judicious search for the true facts of Irish history in his *History of Ireland* was an implicit political riposte to Froude's Hibernophobia, and none the worse for that. Once again, disinterestedness itself could serve a political end.

The *History of Ireland in the Eighteenth Century* reveals Anglo-Irish tensions with which we are by now familiar. Lecky deeply disapproves of the penal laws, castigates absenteeism and registers the suffering of the common people with remarkable sensitivity; but he

72

is reluctant to lay much blame at the door of the Ascendancy, and impugns both British misrule and Irish insurgency. What he dreads most is the danger, foreseen by his beloved Grattan, that 'the ignorant and excitable Catholic population might be one day detached from the influence of property and respectability, and might become a prey to designing agitators and demagogues'.[97] This, of course, is precisely what has come about with the Land League, the Land Acts (which he saw as acts of gross daylight robbery) and Parnell – a sad decline from O'Connell in Lecky's view, which in his terms at the time is hardly saying much. Praised for his equipoise and sagaciousness, as well as for his imaginative empathy with an opponent's case, Lecky's turn to Unionism and opposition to Home Rule really dates from the time of the Land League, in which his own interests as a landlord came under siege. His view that a-rational forces and interests can always be found lurking beneath rational argument was thus triumphantly vindicated by his own behaviour.

'In the existing conditions of Ireland', Lecky writes, 'no Parliament could be established there which could be trusted to fulfil the most elementary conditions of honest government'.[98] Parnell and his cohorts are guilty of 'an amount of intimidation, of cruelty, of systematic disregard for individual freedom scarcely paralleled in any country during the present century'.[99] It is to such discriminating judgements that political interests lead even the most loftily transcendent of minds. Some of the fruits of Lecky's decline into political reaction can be found in his late essays in *Democracy and Liberty* (1896), a volume which includes in its brief, highly negative history of socialism a rare nineteenth-century Irish allusion to Marx's theory of surplus value. His earlier philosophical antipathy to utilitarianism has now narrowed to a distaste for its democratic ethics, which justify the masses in riding roughshod over minorities in hot pursuit of the greatest happiness. The work's two volumes represent some nine hundred pages of reactionary rant against priests, the Land League, democracy and the New Unionism, though he surprisingly puts in the odd progressive word for women. His last monograph, the leaden, sententious *The Map of Life* (1899), is really a moral sermon.

All this can be contrasted with Lecky's youthful, elegantly wrought study *Public Opinion in Ireland*, in which he appears as a Protestant nationalist as well as a stylist of great distinction. A highly idealized cameo of Henry Grattan is followed by one of O'Connell, from whose career those features more palatable to a Grattanite Whig are diplomatically retrieved. O'Connell was not a demagogue or tool of the Catholic clergy, though he could be scurrilous and foul-mouthed enough; he was a religious tolerationist opposed to socialism and insurrectionary violence, and his monster meetings are romantically portrayed. When it comes to pre-Grattanite eighteenth-century Ireland, Lecky's hyperbole knows no bounds: it is 'scarcely possible to conceive a more infamous system of legal tyranny'.[100] It is this erstwhile enthusiast for Young Ireland who will later speak on anti-Home Rule platforms in Britain. Lecky later altered *Public Opinion in Ireland* to adapt the text to his evolving anti-nationalist views, and those opinions were in the end not so different from the elitist, imperialist, illiberal and anti-democratic precepts he had earlier countered in Froude and Carlyle. There is a malignant disloyalty in Ireland, the elderly Lecky warned, and its people are growing dangerously educated and literate.[101]

········

Not all erstwhile enlightened Irish thinkers declined in their twilight years into political apoplexy. If the political intelligence of Ferguson, Lawless, de Vere and others gradually sank, along with the fortunes of their class, into a crudely formulaic Toryism, the extraordinary Standish O'Grady dramatically reversed this direction. His *The Story of Ireland* (1894) is hostile to the monastic spirit, idealizes the Norsemen as hardy Carlylean heroes and admires Cromwell, though not his massacre at Drogheda. Puritan Protestants conquered the island because they were braver and more truthful than the natives, but the penal laws are nevertheless to be condemned. The book sets its face against both the United Irishmen and the Union (an 'abject betrayal'): the Ascendancy should have maintained their power rather than cravenly surrendering it to Westminster. The Repeal movement was 'fraudulent and theatrical', and O'Connell a liar and a fraud, but he was possessed of a great heart. Fintan Lalor was the finest of the Young Irelanders, though O'Grady recommends his mentor Carlyle as an antidote to him. The typical ambiguities of the Anglo-Irish populist are present in plenty.[102]

In O'Grady's political pamphleteering of the 1880s, those contradictions have locked into an almost unthinkable impasse. On the one hand, he declares his belief that 'there will never be an aristocracy . . . so rotten [as the Ascendancy] in its seeming strength, so recreant, resourceless, and stupid in the day of trial, so degenerate, outworn and effete'.[103] The Irish landowners are 'few, friendless, hated, and imbecile', having abnegated their rule to 'a hungry, greedy, anarchic *canaille*'.[104] But no sooner has he written them off with one hand than he is busy refurbishing them with the other, with feudalist fantasies of a revamped landowning oligarchy securing the fealty of its loyal retainers. In 1882, the landlords are 'the noblest and best [class] on Irish soil . . . the highest moral element';[105] in 1886 they are to be brusquely discarded; in 1897 they are wheeled out again and dusted down, as 'the rightful natural leaders, defenders and champions of this People who cannot furnish forth such from their own ranks'.[106] The final phrase is telling: the common people cannot breed their own ready-made organic intellectuals, which is why traditional figures like himself must step into the breach. It is as though Davitt, Parnell and William O'Brien had simply never emerged. O'Grady is too intelligent to believe in the landlords, and too ideological not to.

In his final years, however, O'Grady was to turn tail yet again. After 1900, he becomes interested in Fourier, Tolstoy, Kropotkin and Henry George, advocates communes and begins to call himself a communist – though not a socialist, socialism being a degenerate product of modernity. (He was, however, a champion of that rather less avant-garde variety of the creed, Guild Socialism.) In this bizarre figure, neo-feudalist elitism finally meets up with modern-day anarchism, taking a last impetuous turn to the political left. Both creeds are at one in their hostility to liberal individualism and the industrial middle class. It was thus that the leader writer of the most conservative newspaper in Ireland, the *Express*, graduated to running his own idiosyncratically leftist journal, the *All Ireland Review*. For the panegyrist of Cuchulain to end up only a few yards from the camp of James Connolly is a sign of just how calamitous the crisis in Ireland has grown.

3

Savants and Society

In his *History of European Morals*, W. E. H. Lecky commends medical science as a discipline from which 'the most splendid results might be expected', and remarks of the close relation between mind and body that 'he who raises moral pathology to a science . . . will probably take a place among the master intellects of mankind'.[1] Such a master intellect was in fact just about to loom over the horizon, even if Sigmund Freud's concern was not exactly with 'moral pathology'. Indeed, there is a frail connection between Freud and Dublin medicine: the Irish physician George Sigerson translated Charcot's *Diseases of the Nervous System*, a work which forms part of the early Freud's intellectual background.

It is no accident that a Dublin historian should have had such admiration for medicine, given that the capital was one of its major European intellectual homes. In fact it has been ranked as the third most illustrious city for medicine in the world after Paris and Edinburgh.[2] Davis Coakley remarks that 'the medical world of Dublin was extensive, active, and relatively powerful',[3] and one commentator describes Robert James Graves and William Stokes as 'the founders of British clinical teaching'.[4] Graves, who had travelled in

Europe with the artist J. M. Turner, delivered clinical lectures which were renowned throughout Europe. He worked for a while as a doctor in fever-infested Galway, and gave his name to the exophthalmic goitre; thousands of patients may have owed their lives to his research.[5] There was an intriguingly high number of medical men among the city's intelligentsia: Cheyne, Corrigan, Wilde, Stokes, Graves, Sigerson, Lever.[6] Like the church and the bar, medicine was a vocation for gentlemen, so that the prominence of physicians in Anglo-Irish Dublin was hardly surprising. The Dublin medical profession was almost entirely under Protestant control, with three medical schools staffed exclusively by Protestants, with the lonely exception of one Trinity Catholic.

But medicine is also the most humane and socially minded of the hard sciences, a link between scholarly research and human welfare, and thus peculiarly suited to an intelligentsia which had brains and a social conscience in equal measure. Like antiquarianism, medicine forms a connection between science and society, as the physician combines erudition with worldliness. Health is a matter of the body's interaction with its environment, and so shades off through issues of social reform into political questions. It is thus no accident that William Wilde was medical scientist and antiquarian together: both apparently arcane pursuits have an immediate bearing on social and political life. That Wilde explored the beauties of County Galway but also made forays into fever-ridden slums is by no means incongruous. (His investigations of poverty did not require him to walk far: Merrion Square was cheek-by-jowl with some of the most appalling slums in Europe.) The antiquarian who takes an interest in the 'folk' is also the doctor who busies himself with the common people. Romantic idealism and practical science are linked by a humanitarian ethics.

Medicine, which brought in its wake questions of poverty, sanitation, slum conditions, political interests and the like, thus suited the 'generalist' bent of the Anglo-Irish intellectual. In classical intellectual style, it also provided a bridge between two senses of culture: culture as intellectual work, and culture as a form of social life. As dispensers of advice, succour and consolation, physicians formed a kind of secular clergy whose ministrations could be rather more

77

precious than those of the priests. As Charles Lever writes, 'No other class whose minds are trained by a course of labour, have so many opportunities of mixing with their fellow-men of every grade as the physician'.[7] The clergy, Lever comments, are forbidden worldly involvements, whereas the lawyer has far too many, viewing the world as just 'one wide arena of litigation'. But the medic's position 'will put him in relations of warm feelings and sympathies' with every condition of life, allowing him to obtain 'a deep insight into the world and its ways' but also into the 'secret workings of the mind in every derangement of the body'.[8] Not surprisingly, Lever makes the physician sound just like the novelist. The other professions may be overstocked, as Lever imagines the nation 'thatching their barns with unemployed barristers and making corduroy roads with idle curates',[9] but it is rare to hear of a surplus of doctors.

Besides, medicine, rather like political economy, was struggling at the time to establish itself as a bona fide academic discipline, and stressing its social dimension could help in this respect. Even one of the subject's most illustrious Irish practitioners, William Stokes, denied it the status of an exact science. It could thus win itself a degree of reputability by hooking up with other, more well-accredited pursuits. The practice of law, rather similarly, was both academic and political. A barrister like Isaac Butt could contribute precisely as a lawyer to political questions such as land tenure and tenants' rights, while his nationalist ideas were reinforced by his professional pursuit of defending Fenians in court.

········

The Stokes family formed one of the mighty Irish intellectual dynasties. William Stokes's father, the physician and political thinker Whitley Stokes, was a Gaelic scholar who published an Irish–English dictionary, wrote poetry and took an interest in natural history and mineralogy. His home in Dublin's Harcourt Street was a familiar venue for artists and intellectuals. A cousin, George Gabriel Stokes, was Lucasian Professor of Mathematics at Cambridge and pioneered the modern theory of viscous fluids, while an uncle was a Fellow of Trinity College. Whitley Stokes was briefly a member of the United Irishmen, indeed drafted a plan of parliamentary reform for their Dublin branch. He was penalized for this association by Dublin University, but finally broke with the group over the question of violence. Wolfe Tone called him 'the very best man I have ever known'.[10] In his *Projects for Re-establishing the Internal Peace and Tranquillity of Ireland*, published one year after the United Irish rebellion, Stokes notes that 'fifty thousand of our countrymen have been cut off, a great part of the artificial property of five counties destroyed',[11] but deals largely with agrarian rather than political matters. Horrified by United Irish violence and sectarianism, he nevertheless claims to understand their material causes, as a physician who knew the slums of Dublin at first hand. The uprising must be firmly set in the context of popular suffering, and what strikes some as idleness is in fact unemployment.

The trashy romantic reading-matter of the lower classes has stirred them fatefully to revolt, fostering a spirit of war and vengeance; and Stokes, who holds that 'nothing but mutual forgiveness can save Ireland',[12] wants to oust this dangerous kitsch with manuals on farming, natural history and the like. The Catholic Church should scrap Latin and replace it with Irish, while the clergy should appoint themselves 'friends of the poor, live in their houses, share their potatoes, be their advisors'.[13] From his intimate acquaintance with the atrocious conditions of working-class Dublin, this devoutly religious,[14] compassionate reformer emerges as a stalwart apologist for the poor and paints a graphic portrait of their destitution. As a champion of the lower classes, Stokes also launched a swingeing, eloquent critique of Malthusian theory, which for him meant nothing but mischief in Ireland. From Malthus's viewpoint, workhouses, hospitals, inoculations and the rest 'can only prolong the wretched lives of those who should have been dead long ago, or indeed should never have been born'.[15] With the brisk practicality of his class, Stokes advances instead schemes for bog drainage and agricultural reform.

As a scholar equally well versed in High Crosses and the price of a Dublin lodging house, Whitley Stokes was an appropriate father for his polymath son William. Stokes Junior, who alongside his medical labours translated the New Testament into Irish and was co-founder of the Dublin zoological gardens, worked as a physician during the Famine and witnessed a good many workhouse horrors.[16] He was also devoted to music, natural history, the fine arts and archaeology, and Mahaffy comments that his home was 'the resort of all the wit and all the learning which Ireland possessed'.[17] A fine anecdotalist and conversationalist, Stokes was no slouch at wit himself, remarking of a Trinity don that 'he has a thing called his wife and things called his children, but he was never married'. Thomas Carlyle's dyspeptic account of his tour of Ireland finds the Stokes *ménage* rather less appealing: Stokes himself he portrays as a 'clever, energetic, but squinting, rather fierce, sinister-looking man', while his wife is a 'dim Glasgow lady' who 'bored me to excess'.[18] Stokes studied medicine in Glasgow and Edinburgh and won celebrity with a treatise on chest diseases; he was also an early champion of the stethoscope, by which, as he observed, 'the eye is converted into an ear', and wrote the first account of it in English. He became Regius Professor of Medicine at Dublin University and later president of the Royal Irish Academy. Lady Ferguson wrote of him with exquisite tact that 'the tenderness of his nature and his brilliant wit and humour were only manifested on occasion'.[19]

Stokes conceived of his profession with the typically voluminous humanism of the Anglo-Irish scholar. He was a tireless advocate of an arts education for medical students,[20] and viewed medicine as 'no solitary science, but rather a complex system of knowledge of various kinds, derived from many sources', in which law and mathematics, divinity and physics played their essential parts.[21] The chief evil of the medical profession, he considered, was the confounding of instruction with education, cramming the student with technical knowledge while neglecting his general culture. Whether one would really prefer a physician who knew more about Mozart than multiple sclerosis is perhaps questionable; but Stokes, as a traditional intellectual, is scornful of the philistine specialism of the professional one, and sees just how it sequesters him from the very people he is supposed to serve. A humane education thus has desirable political consequences, as the convergence of several disciplines leads to the convergence of the classes. Medicine is an inexact science, but since ethics and divinity are too, this is hardly a reproach to it. On the hospital wards, the medical student learns courage, mercy and compassion, which is more than he picks up in the lecture theatre.[22]

If medicine connected the disciplines, it also formed a pivot between science and society. Stokes was a pioneer of public health and state medicine, and comes close in his writings to what one might call a sociology of the body. The theory of preventative medicine involves a new kind of social totalization, stretching from state institutions to the domestic hearth, sanitation to standards of living, professional occupations to the duties of property. It battles against 'ignorance, selfishness, the grinding of the poor, the consumption of human life, like fuel, for the production of wealth and vicious indulgence'.[23] It is, in short, an unavoidably political pursuit. Just as the state of the nation lent a political resonance to the study of history, so its backward social conditions forced medicine into the domain of politics. As far as Stokes was concerned, it also raised philosophical and theological questions: Why was there disease at all? Was it on account of the Fall? National health is ineluctably bound up with national morality and prosperity: it will only be fully secured by a social order in which 'no man for his own ends or his profit will be permitted to damage the health or well-being of his neighbour or of his servant'.[24] Medicine thus becomes political critique, not least for a patrician-minded, non-commercial bourgeoisie who looked down benevolently on the people while looking askance at their own less humanitarian business colleagues.

In the manner of his caste, however, Stokes's radicalism was strictly limited. He opposed church disestablishment, and though a supporter of Catholic emancipation, shared the well-nigh universal Anglo-Irish animus against O'Connell. Though he admired Thomas Davis and was a friend of Isaac Butt, he viewed Young Ireland as a degradation and set his face against Home Rule. The true martyrs of the Famine, he once remarked with egregious insensitivity, were the Irish landowners. He was to play his part in perpetuating the Stokes dynasty by producing Margaret Stokes, a Celtic scholar who published a sober, lucid, judicious work, *Early Christian Architecture in Ireland* (1878), a notable physician son, William, and Whitley Stokes Junior, a Celtic and Sanskrit scholar of exceptional distinction much lauded by Matthew Arnold in his *On the Study of Celtic Literature*. Stokes has been commended on the most prodigious achievement in Old and Middle Irish of anyone of his time.[25] He was also author of a magisterial two-volume work, *The Anglo-Indian Codes* (1888–9), in which he performs the gargantuan colonialist labour of codifying English law in India. He has performed this task, he comments in his introduction, not only for the sake of judges, law students and the like, but for bankers, trader, public servants and 'all who take an interest in the efforts of English statesmen to confer on India the blessings of a wise, clear, and ascertainable law'.[26] Samuel Ferguson describes Whitley Stokes as 'one of the leading authorities in Celtic and old Irish philology in all the universities of Europe', author of many precious volumes 'of which the noisy Irish know nothing'.[27] Popular disloyalty for Ferguson evidently extended to ignoring some highly esoteric Celtic philology as well as the laws of the land.

....

Much the same capacious humanism characterizes the work of William Stokes's medical colleague William Wilde. Though Lord Alfred Douglas wrote spitefully of him that he ran a chemist's shop, he was probably the most many-sided intellectual of all. Wilde was a member of learned societies in Paris, Berlin, Vienna and Athens, and his colossal erudition in botany and zoology could well have qualified him as a natural historian. He wrote some original papers in biology, not least on the nipples of the whale. A superb popularizer, he lectured for the Royal Dublin Society on a range of topics, from fishes' gizzards to the unrolling of mummies, and was among other pursuits a distinguished folklorist, archaeologist, ethnologist and antiquarian. Topographical works like *The Beauties of the Boyne* (1849) fluently interpenetrate history and geography. As a medical historian as well as an eminent physician, he somehow found time to edit the *Dublin Journal of Medical Science Quarterly*. He was appointed medical census commissioner in 1841, and brought to the task a mania for minutely detailed description; Terence de Vere White thinks his census report should be catalogued alongside such baroque literary flights as Richard Burton's *Anatomy of Melancholy* and Sir Thomas Browne's *Urn Burial*.[28] He also took part in the census of 1851, meticulously handwriting the two volumes of the report on disease and death and gaining himself a knighthood in the process. The work has been described as one of the greatest demographic studies ever conducted.[29]

Famed as the dirtiest man in Dublin, as well as for his wit and conversational prowess, Wilde catalogued the antiquities in the Royal Irish Academy and became Surgeon Oculist to the Queen in Ireland. He is also reported to have operated on the eyes of the king of Sweden, and when the king was temporarily blinded to have seduced his queen. 'Wilde's incision' is still used in mastoid surgery, and he also bestowed his name on a condition of the inner ear. He was one of the finest aurists of his day, and wrote the first important textbook on aural surgery. His early work on medicine in Austria contains some detailed, rather dull accounts of surgical operations, but typically fans out to take in the history and culture of Austria.[30] Invited as a young physician to play medical advisor to a gentleman voyager, he recorded his overseas adventures in a colourful, stylishly executed travel book which praises Egyptian slavery; the slaves, he argues, are better fed and clothed than free servants.[31]

Wilde's treatise on deafness and mutism suggests something of the less-than-exact state of the medical science of his day. The mute, he considers, is 'degraded by his uncontrollable passions' and little above a beast.[32] Most of Ireland's 'mutes' seem congregated in its mountainous coastal regions, and in Switzerland, with its low, damp valleys and poor diet, they are unsurprisingly prevalent. Fright during pregnancy, Wilde speculates, may be a possible cause of the ailment. The work pulls together his scientific and anecdotal talents, sprinkled as it is with a number of tales of 'mutism', and as a work of medical sociology follows in the wake of his rather more celebrated study of Swift's supposed insanity. Breezily announcing that 'we do not acknowledge the narrow limits which are usually assigned to what is called medicine',[33] he records his partly phrenological investigations of the Dean's skull, which resembles that of a 'Celtic aborigine'. Medicine and patriotism are thus yoked conveniently together.

Wilde's explorations of the Celtic aborigine largely took the form of folklore. *Irish Popular Superstitions*, written with florid romanticism in the wake of the Famine, has the consciously commemorative function of preserving what he sees as an almost defunct popular culture, a flamboyantly rollicking world whose waning he greets with paternalist regret. He records this dying culture in some vivid cameos, as a kind of minor novelist *manqué*. Unlike his rather less tender-hearted wife, an enthusiast for the Antipodes, he mourns the fact of Irish emigration, believing as he does that the country is unequally rather than over-populated; but though he launches some mild criticism of the landlords, he also looks with dismay on a Europe seized by revolutionary turmoil. If one part of his mind is away with the elves, the other is with an honest, open-hearted, industrious Englishness, which will put an end to the falseness and indolence of his native land. In a familiar Ascendancy tension between culture and politics, it is unclear how his zest for this soberly disciplined regime can coexist with a nostalgia for fairies and holy wells.

Workhouse mortality, Wilde comments, is running at a rate which beggars belief, but he is reluctant to excite 'angry feelings' against these institutions. Agrarian agitators are 'pot-house demagogues and idle malcontents', duping the gullible tenantry. Though he is keen on the cultural self-expression of the common people, he is distinctly more wary of their political self-manifestation. Elsewhere, he approves of emigration on the idiosyncratic grounds that it permits the hardy Celt to help build great empires elsewhere, but exhorts the less imperially minded Irish who stay behind to learn 'a love of truth, cleanliness, self-reliance, and a more perfect system of agriculture'.[34] Wilde himself was hardly a shining example of the first two virtues. The Irish, he comments complacently at the height of the Fenian agitation, live 'under the mildest government in the world', where 'all enjoy the blessings of civil and religious liberty'.[35] His later work on Lough Corib opens with the *caveat* that he will not be dealing here with the 'miserably clad spalpeen . . . politics, peelers and parsons . . . Fenians and Repealers', solely with the beauties of Nature.[36] Like much of Wilde's writing, the book is cast in a sprightly, cavalier, deliberately non-academic style. It is the prose of the genteel Irish intellectual, amused, affable and slightly rakish, which is averse to specialism and wears its learning with a light, insouciant air.

········

The link between the medical community of Victorian Dublin and the Irish Revival is the Ulsterman George Sigerson, who wrote on paralysis and St Patrick, Norse Ireland and the advantages of ambidexterity.[37] Born near Strabane seven years after Catholic Emancipation, Sigerson lived long enough to be appointed a senator of the Irish Free State. He was also a fellow of the Royal University, professor of biology at University College, Dublin and president of the National Library Society. In his spare time he was a poet, a member of the Irish Literary Society and a Royal Commissioner for prisons. His works mark the point where the tradition of Protestant liberalism is beginning to shift decisively towards Gaelic nationalism. *Modern Ireland*, in liberal fashion, insists on the country's ethnic mix (Sigerson was himself of Irish-Danish stock), and speaks up proudly for the lineage of non-Gaelic political leadership in Ireland: 'From Silken Thomas to James Stephens, the Normans and Saxons, the Cromwellians and Williamites have contributed their quota, and more than their quota, to the number of insurgent leaders'.[38] While not numbering himself in these revolutionary ranks, he believes in the wake of the Manchester martyrs that Fenianism must be seriously attended to, as the product of an Irish scepticism about pleading their case by constitutional means to a resolutely deaf Britain. Briskly dispelling some British illusions on the matter, he points to the tenacity and democratic character of the Fenian movement. While not wholly idealizing ancient land tenures, he contrasts the non-absolute power of the Gaelic chieftain with what he sees as the autocratic rule of the present-day landlord, and paints a colourful, lopsided portrait of the gentry as drunken and corrupt. But he also lambasts O'Connell's treatment of the forty-shilling freeholders, and elevates the hardy democratic spirit of Ulster over the temper of the rest of the island. The range of the work, from law, emigration and education to medicine and the Irish convict system, reflects the familiar encylopaedism of the Irish Victorian scholar.

Like others we have examined, Sigerson is caught on the hop between judicious all-roundedness and partisan sympathies. It is just that in his case the partisanship is now nationalist rather than Unionist. He writes with restraint on the land question, hopeful that Gladstone's Land Act will pave the way to class-harmony and allow landowners to cultivate cordial relations with their tenantry. Though he supports tenant proprietorship, he sees it as somehow equably coexisting with the landlord system. His nationalist historiography, however, is rather less modulated. *The Last Independent Parliament of Ireland* (1919), admittedly the work of an octogenarian, is for the most part stage-nationalist bombast which attributes all Irish instability to British rule, sees the penal laws as the 'black code of Anti-Christ'[39] and commends the nation with a cavalier flourish on its unparalleled fighting record. His most vital contribution to the Revival was his *Bards of the Gael and Gall* (1897), at once an impressive piece of scholarship and an advanced case of Gaelic literary chauvinism. Sigerson thinks the Celts introduced rhyme, blank verse, romances, the hymn, the mock-heroic, the first poems of exile and the first patriotic verses into post-classical literature, and regards Ireland as having 'develop[ed] the literary instinct or culture of other nations'.[40] The penal laws tried to 'annihilate the intellect of a people that had generally fostered the development of all other peoples, and liberally enlightened the world'.[41] Whether Celtic epic was the source for Tibetan poetry passes unexamined. Rabelais probably stole from Celtic writing, and Latin picks up some of its qualities; even Tennyson's mode of expression is curiously Gaelic. Ancient Ireland, in brief, is the *fons et origo* of literary styles, genres and devices. Despite this cultural supremicism, he is a genuinely literary cosmopolitan, fascinated by cross-cultural fertilizations rather than just by the unilateral influence of the Irish on a gratefully receptive world.

The Plough and the Stars

Philosophically speaking, upper classes tend to idealism, whereas middle classes incline to empiricism. Those who do little labour can afford to imagine that ideas are autonomous of reality, while those like the industrial middle class who work closer to the ground value experience and experiment, what they can see, taste and handle. The former tend to adhere to innate ideas and *a priori* principles, whereas the latter derive their notions from the dust and heat of practice, cobbling them provisionally together as they go along. If the middle class derides the upper class as remote and ineffectual, the upper class despises the middle class as crass and commonplace. The upper class cannot descend to a practicality, while the middle class cannot rise to an abstraction.

In a brilliant essay on William Rowan Hamilton, David Attis shows how this ideological context informs the apparently quite value-free matter of his work on conical refraction. Since that work rested entirely on mathematical calculations which still waited upon experimental proof, it was a triumph for the more rationalist, deductive or conservative school of science, and a rebuff to Hamilton's more progressive, empiricist rivals such as the Whig Dissenters Henry Brougham and David Brewster. Hamilton's friend Aubrey de Vere acclaimed his discovery as showing 'reason harnessed as leader in these utilitarian times'.[42] 'Utilitarian' is de Vere's shorthand for the middle-class ideology which in Ireland finds another outlet in political nationalism; indeed, he and Hamilton often discussed their mutual fear of utilitarian theory, sharing the belief that only some form of metaphysical idealism would redeem the nation from this destructive doctrine. O'Connell had been a Benthamite, in fact corresponded with Bentham for a time, and the Tory Hamilton was resolutely opposed to Repeal. The utilitarian tenet that social institutions were simply contrivances of social convenience struck deep at the conservative Ascendancy faith that they were founded on *a priori* metaphysical principles and ordained by the Almighty.[43]

De Vere's political term 'leader' is significant: what Hamilton had demonstrated by a highly esoteric piece of physics was the sovereignty of reason over empirical labour, which can be politically translated as the dominance of timeless conservative principles over more experience-dependent (and so relative) ones. In conducting the work, Hamilton was also keen to promote Anglo-Irish relations by showing Irish science to be capable of major accomplishments, thus strengthening the Union at the level of intellectual theory. His magnificent achievement in the field of conical refraction stands of course by its scientific merits, and there is no suggestion that his motive in carrying it out was in the least ideological. But its reception is yet another reminder that Anglo-Irish disinterestedness was not always quite as untainted as it appeared.

Hamilton is said, perhaps hyperbolically, to have studied Hebrew, Latin, Persian, Sanskrit, Arabic, Chaldee and Syriac as a child, wrote poetry later and was congratulated by his friend William Wordsworth on penning verses 'animated with true poetic spirit'.[44] Wordsworth added that his poetry lacked something in workmanship, which counts as one of the literary understatements of the nineteenth century. Wordsworth visited Ireland in 1829 at Hamilton's invitation, and on arriving in the country went first to the astronomer's observatory. A regular correspondent of Wordsworth, Coleridge and Maria Edgeworth, Hamilton took a keen interest in German aesthetics and metaphysics, and philosophically speaking was a Kantian of sorts. Wordsworth declared that he was like Coleridge, a dubious compliment at best. He was appointed Astronomer Royal of Ireland[45] and elected president of the Royal Irish Academy, where with a touch of smugness he produced a phrenological analysis of his own character. He wrote of his knighthood that 'it was so absolutely *unsought for*, yet appears so *natural*'.[46]

Hamilton's greatest contribution to mathematics was the discovery in 1843, while pacing Dublin's Grand Canal, of quaternions, which involve a combination of real and imaginary numbers and constitute an entirely new mathematical language. Since this allows any line in any direction in space to be transformed into any other, it is uncannily prescient of Einsteinian physics. His book on the subject sold no copies at all in Ireland, and only one other academic, Tait of Edinburgh, is said to have been able to understand it. Hamilton also teetered on the brink of discovering quantum mechanics, and some contemporary mathematicians express surprise that he did not.[47] Hamilton passed through the Famine and its aftermath with his head rather guiltily in the clouds, preoccupied with such pressing questions as how long it took Christ to ascend into heaven, and the physical location of heaven itself.[48] His remoteness seems even unwittingly to have infiltrated others' appreciative comments on him: 'He stood so high', wrote Samuel Ferguson, 'that all who looked up at all saw and recognised his pre-eminence'.[49] He was said to have lived in a 'state of perpetual cerebral excitement'.[50]

Hamilton was a prime example of Gramsci's traditional intellectual. It is not hard to believe that mathematical truths are eternal, and the epistemological rationalism with which they were in his view linked had distinctively conservative implications. A fellow Irish astronomer, the Earl of Rosse, who had the honour of allowing Lady Gregory to peer up his telescope, saw in science the kind of common ground for a fissiparous nation that others ascribed to culture. In science, Rosse writes, 'the mind is carried . . . beyond and far above the petty and ephemeral contests of this life'.[51] It is the authentic note of the Anglo-Irish liberal. The natural scientist, by contrast, fits the category of organic intellectual rather better. Gramsci, as we have seen, includes political organizers under that heading, but he also has in mind those intellectuals who work in more direct relation to the material world, scientists, technicians and administrators who play a key role in the development of production and who are thus less likely to regard their own ideas as Platonically immutable. In this sense, natural scientists rank among the most powerful organic intellectuals of the emergent middle class, concerned as it is to overturn a world of self-validating *a priori* notions, apply ideas to the ends of social progress and treat knowledge as a dynamic force of production.

Roy Johnston has argued that, around the time of the Ordnance Survey, there was in Ireland 'a strong, optimistic and, in a sense, patriotic scientific culture'.[52] Originating in the pre-Union *belle epoque*, it rose to a pre-Famine peak which was symbolized by the meeting in Cork in 1843 of the British Association for the Advancement of Science. The Royal Dublin Society aspired to be a kind of university of technology, an analogue of the *École Polytechnique* of Paris. And Trinity had a reasonably enlightened curriculum, equipped with the physical and biological sciences by the mid-century. At a Dublin convention of the British Association in 1835, where the presidential address was delivered by Hamilton, a clear third of the papers in mathematics, physics and chemistry were from Irish participants.

Johnston notes that basic mathematics, including some surveying, had been taught in the traditional Irish hedge schools; in fact, the eighteenth-century Clare poet Brian Merriman was a surveyor, and the physicist John Tyndall was inducted into surveying at a Carlow hedge school, thus later qualifying for recruitment to the Ordnance Survey. But the national movement, so Johnston considers, showed little interest in the relevance of science and technology to nation-building, as Young Ireland's Romantic anti-utilitarianism would testify. An unsigned piece in the *Nation,* which could be from the pen of Thomas Davis, elevates Puseyism, Merrie England and Disraeli's Young England over the Benthamites and technologists of modernity. In response to an Irish bishop's euphoric claim that the nation holds up on her coastline the cross of faith in one hand and the torch of science in the other, the indefatigably anti-clerical William Ryan observed that 'we devoutly wish that she would turn [the torch of science] now and then on her own children'.[53]

Even so, nineteenth-century Ireland was home to a distinguished lineage of scientists, from the great John Tyndall to the astronomer the Earl of Rosse and the eminent chemist Robert Kane. Rosse's son invented the steam turbine, and the country also produced the inventor of the induction coil and the industrial electromagnet.[54] Richard Griffith, father of Irish geology, executed what remains to this day one of the finest geological maps ever produced, while Robert Mallat's Royal Irish Academy paper of 1846 on earthquake tremors laid the foundations for modern seismology. George Salmon's treatise on conic sections was to remain the definitive work on the subject for half a century. There was to be an upsurge in Irish science around the first decade of the twentieth century, with a flood of publications on collembola.[55] John Tyndall, born in Carlow but a resident of England for most of his life, studied in Marburg, became a Fellow of the Royal Society and wrote on a wide range of topics, from heat, light and the motion of glaciers (he was an accomplished mountaineer) to radiation and bacteria. A life-long colleague of Faraday, he ended up as professor of natural philosophy at the Royal Institute of London.[56] He died from an overdose of chloral, mistakenly administered to him by his wife.

Science in nineteenth-century Ireland remained very much the domain of the Ascendancy, 'the cultural property of a powerful section of society to enhance its claims to the guardianship of enlightened cultural interests and to promote its particular ethos'.[57] It was, in short, still largely the province of a traditional rather than an organic intelligentsia; its key institutions, the Royal Dublin Society and the Royal Irish Academy, represented 'the intellectual foci of the Protestant colonial nation, basically the landed gentry and the Trinity College elite, with very little enrichment from the rising Catholic middle classes'.[58] Tyndall himself, despite his deeply controversial agnosticism, was a fervent Unionist who detested Gladstone and held in the fashion of the traditional intellectual that scientific investigation should be free of utilitarian ends. If he was an intellectual progressive, he was a political conservative. If the country lacked a large enough technical intelligentsia to challenge the sway of the Ascendancy, it was partly because it lacked the material means to produce a sizeable stratum of chemists, biologists, engineers and the like. George Russell claimed that a rural society will tend to breed literary intellectuals since it lacks the industrial diversity to produce a more complex, specialized intelligentsia.[59] He was himself a fine example of his theory, linking poetry and dairy production in his own person. Given the minor status of the industrial middle class outside north-east Ulster, traditional intellectuals thus played a more prominent role in Ireland than is customary in a more advanced social order. They also bulked unusually large in nineteenth-century England, partly because the industrial middle class was content to leave cultural (and to some extent political) leadership in the hands of their social superiors. But they were hardly so pre-eminent in science.

No doubt the Catholic Church's nervousness of free inquiry played a part in this tardy development of a Catholic intelligentsia, along with Catholics' greater educational disabilities. The bishops' rejection of the Queen's colleges may well have set back Catholic education for two generations, with some devastating consequences in particular for the Catholic contribution to science and technology. The Catholic scientists Kane and Callan were educated respectively in Germany and Italy. One might also claim that Catholic scholastic theology is rationalist rather than empiricist in bent, a matter of adjusting the world to certain first principles rather than vice versa. It is thus not especially hospitable to rule-of-thumb experiment, not to speak of the necessary open-endedness of the scientific hypothesis. Almost all Irish scientists stemmed from the Protestant middle class, with rather more professionals among them than in genteel-amateur England – a sign of the way in which Irish scientific research was dominated by public institutions (the Museum of Irish Industry, the Department of Science and Arts, the Royal College of Science), and through them by a central administration. The state exercised greater control of science in Ireland than in Britain, with scientists receiving annual grants from the government considerably earlier than their English counterparts. It was another instance of the government-funded, centralized intelligentsia of a colonial nation, in which, given the backwardness of civil society, the state tends to assume a high profile in intellectual work and elsewhere. The Queen's colleges had chairs in chemistry, mathematics, mineralogy, geology and natural history; indeed, it was upon science that many of the episcopal charges of godlessness and secularism were focused. The Museum of Economic Geology (1845), later the Museum of Irish Industry, became in 1867 the Royal College of Science for Ireland, with a mandate to stage popular scientific lectures intended among others for the 'artisan class'.[60]

....

One of the most distinguished of Irish scientists, however, was an intellectual of the Catholic reforming middle class, Robert Kane. If his name sounds more English than Gaelic, it was because his father, a United Irishman on the run, had changed it from 'Kean'. Kane Senior was a Dublin chemical manufacturer, and his son got his modest start as a clinical clerk to Stokes and Graves at the Meath hospital. Fifty years later, he was to succeed his mentor Stokes as president of the Royal Irish Academy, to which he himself had been elected at the precocious age of twenty-two. One year earlier, while still an undergraduate at Trinity, he had been elected to the Chair of Chemistry of the Apothecaries' Company, at a time when chemical instruments, according to Sir Robert Boyle, were almost 'unprocurable' in Ireland. It was, Boyle observed, a country in which it was 'hard to have any hermetic thoughts'.[61] Kane launched the first successful scientific periodical of any kind in Ireland, the *Dublin Journal of Medical and Chemical Science* (1831), delivered some extraordinarily popular lectures at the Dublin Royal Society and won himself a European reputation for his work on ammonia compounds. His textbook *Elements of Chemistry* (1840) was the foremost such work of its day, but his masterpiece was *The Industrial Resources of Ireland* (1844), nominated by one ecstatic reviewer as 'the most important work which has ever issued from the Irish press'.[62] It is a magisterial work of scholarship which spans everything from turf and railways to canals and fertilizers, a remarkable harnessing of geography, geology, mineralogy and a whole gamut of academic disciplines to the 'national' cause. Kane was not himself a nationalist; indeed, he was a convinced Unionist opposed to Parnell and Home Rule. But in claiming that Ireland had the resources for economic self-sufficiency, his study buttressed the political case of his nationalist Catholic colleagues, whatever his intentions. Thomas Davis reviewed it glowingly in the *Nation*,[63] another instance of the liaison between the intellectual and the activist.

Kane, typically enough in nineteenth-century Ireland, was a kind of state intellectual. He was involved in the Ordnance Survey, and became director of a geological museum set up by Sir Robert Peel. He was also one of the government commissioners appointed to inquire into the potato blight during the Famine. As a commissioner for national education, he was requested by the Lord Lieutenant to prepare a survey of higher education in Europe, and his report was used in drawing up the charter and statutes of the Queen's colleges. He was, in short, a typically versatile Irish intellectual who moved easily between academia and the public sphere. His inaugural address as president of University College Cork cannily counteracts the 'godless' charge levelled at the Queen's colleges by making heavy weather of the college's moral guardianship of its students. Education must be for the 'actual world in which we live', and science reveals the 'glorious evidence of infinite goodness'.[64] It was an astute blend of the holy and the hard-headed, rallying science to the banner of eternal life. Isaac Butt achieved much the same delicate equipose of organic and traditional in an address to a popular educational institute in Limerick, paying homage to the technical uses of knowledge while insisting on such learning as an end in itself.[65]

Modern languages and the natural sciences, Kane insists, will be central to the Cork college, given the 'wretchedly low standards of literary and scientific education amongst our people'.[66] He is a modernizing rather than traditional intellectual, as preoccupied with the cultural destiny of the Catholic masses as with ammonia compounds, and intent on an alliance between the two. Taking a discreet side-smack at Trinity, he complains that there has been no Irish seat of learning which might provide an intellectual centre for the people,[67] though he then dextrously pulls back from the charge of populist pragmatism. Abstract learning is an excellent thing, and he 'cannot conceive any thing more narrow and degrading than an absorption into the mere details of practical existence'.[68] It is an adroit balancing act between Newman and Cullen, Lecky and O'Connell. The only hope of redeeming the parlous condition of the nation lies in the diffusion of practical knowledge among its people. This, with its ardour for industrial education and popular knowledge, is a markedly different project from that of the traditional Anglo-Irish intelligentsia, but its political purpose lies close to their own. The Queen's colleges will create unity and harmony among all sects and parties, so that all 'may learn to know and love each other'.[69] Despite this eirenic vision, Kane was later to be fingered as the culprit when a mysterious fire burned down part of the college of which he was president. In order to placate the Vatican's suspicions of the Queen's colleges, he diplomatically ensured that his Cork address was translated into Italian. The translator, however, a somewhat shady professor of Italian at Trinity, mistranslated a good deal of the text, substituting for its opening phrase 'Ladies and Gentlemen' the words 'Gentlemen of both sexes'. Reading this, a Vatican cardinal was moved to remark that 'Cork must be a queer city', little knowing how proleptic his adjective was to prove.[70] At the age of eighty, Kane was busily translating Scott's *Ivanhoe* into Spanish.

Kane had had an illustrious eighteenth-century predecessor in

Richard Kirwan, a chemist held in hardly less esteem than the great Lavoisier himself. He produced a pioneering study of the mineralogy of Ireland,[71] and was elected an honorary member of academies in Berlin, Stockholm, Uppsala, Philadelphia, Edinburgh, Jena and Dijon. He was also a fellow of the Royal Society of London, president of the Royal Irish Academy and – the ultimate accolade – a perpetual member of the Amicable Society of Galway. He was also the only person ever granted the privilege of keeping his hat on during the examinations for Trinity fellowships. Kirwan knew Burke, Maria Edgeworth and Joseph Priestley, became a Unitarian and was sworn into the United Irishmen by William James McNevin. He moved in a Dublin well-versed in Rousseau, Deism and the French *philosophes*, and as a scientific polymath was one of the earliest organic intellectuals of Catholic nationalism. His aim, like Kane's later, was to apply science patriotically to national industrial progress, and like Kane he regarded the nation as capable of economic autarky.[72] As a humanist intellectual of varied interests, he found time to pen an essay on human happiness, which in Benthamite fashion identifies happiness with pleasure, and which with much moral platitudinizing provides a compact history of happiness from Adam (who lived to the age of nine hundred and thirty) down through the ages.[73]

If Kane had a prestigious forerunner in Kirwan, he had a renowned acolyte in William K. Sullivan. Born into the Catholic nationalist middle class as the son of a Cork paper mill proprietor, Sullivan studied chemistry in Germany and became Kane's private assistant. He was director of the Museum of Irish Industry, then Chemist to the Museum, then, in succession to his mentor, president of Queen's College Cork. As another state intellectual, he worked for government departments such as the Geology Survey, and was Chemist to the Royal Agricultural Improvement Society. His politics, however, were of a different colour from Kane's. He was involved in the prelude to the 1848 uprising, but was kept out of the event itself by a bout of rheumatic fever; he was also a shareholder in the *Irish Tribune*, the suppressed successor to the also suppressed *United Irishman*. He published jointly with Kane, especially on sugar beet,[74] and rather less prosaically translated parts of a German work of Celtic studies. He was also editor of Eugene O'Curry's epoch-making three-volume work, *On the Manners and Customs of the Ancient Irish* (1873). In fact he was an ancient historian as well as a chemist: when he edited O'Curry's posthumous papers, it is claimed that he had to read more or less the whole manuscript literature of Ireland in order to track down some of O'Curry's unreferenced allusions. Probably a native Irish speaker, he was remarkably learned on the social and political institutions of early Ireland, as well as philology; his daunting linguistic knowledge covered among other tongues Finnish, Turkish and Magyar.

Sullivan, in short, was the integral Irish scholar, and like Kirwan and Kane an 'organic' intellectual who placed knowledge within the context of national development. It is just that whereas the Unionist Kane confined that progress largely to economic matters, Kirwan and Sullivan, as representatives of a rising Catholic middle class, saw it as carrying radical political connotations too. It was impossible for the 'progressive' scientific intellectual not to concern himself with education, politics and society as well as with chemistry or biology. In his *University Education in Ireland*, Sullivan writes as a spirited champion of his class, as well as one conscious of the faintly oxymoronic flavour of the phrase 'Catholic scientist'. Catholicism, he holds defiantly, is compatible with the 'fullest and free cultivation of all human sciences'; the Ascendancy party are aware that 'a properly educated Catholic middle class would soon deprive them of a monopoly [of culture] which they formerly defended in the name of conservatism, but which they now propose to maintain in the name of liberalism and enlightenment'.[75] Genuinely mixed education, he considers, is possible only on the basis of political and religious equality, whereas the Queen's colleges are Protestant in all but name. The emerging middle classes in Ireland lack traditional cultivation, and so are bound to be defective, a flaw which takes the guise of a respectable conformism and a lack of independent thought. It is this defect, at once political and intellectual, that the diffusion of scientific knowledge will help to repair.

In another work, Sullivan provides a detailed sociology of Belgian industrial training institutions for Irish edification. The whole of the skilled industry of Ireland, he claims, has been monopolized by one section of its people: skilled artisans are mostly Protestant, while 'the simplest elements of cookery are unknown to fully three-fourths of the Irish population'.[76] Ireland's colonial history has thus retarded its economic evolution. In Sullivan's view, the great problem of the national schools is one of student absenteeism, as the 'extreme poverty of the people' induces them to keep children at home to work. To remedy this deficiency, he suggests attaching industrial training units to the schools as an incentive for students: academic study would be rewarded by employment in these workshops.

As editor of the *Monthly Journal of Progress*, Sullivan published pieces on art, education, sanitation, libraries, social reform and a range of similar public-spirited topics. Kane contributed to the journal, pleading for a public library in Dublin and village reading rooms to foster a healthy public opinion in the teeth of newspaper trivia and political partisanship. In the popularizing style of the organic intelligentsia, Sullivan delivered public lectures under the joint aegis of the government and the Royal Dublin Society, and in 1856 became professor of chemistry at the Catholic University – an appointment which offended Cardinal Cullen because of Sullivan's nationalist opinions. Newman, who was surprisingly enlightened about science, fitted him up with an expensive laboratory, one of the finest in the country, and both men aimed to develop a comprehensive school of science.[77]

Newman and Sullivan also co-founded *Atlantis*, house-journal of the Catholic University, of which Sullivan became editor in 1858.[78] Topics in the journal ranged from Joan of Arc and the history of the Benedictines to essays on ancient Ireland by Eugene O'Curry, along with – this thankfully by a non-Irish author – the penetration of the ovum by spermatozoa. The periodical cavalierly disregarded the frontiers between academic genres, with D. F. McCarthy on Calderon, essays on the date of the book of Job and Assyrio-Babylonian polyphony, Arabic translations of the Bible and, by Sullivan himself, dolomitic limestone. Sullivan also contributed a highly learned, eccentric and esoteric piece entitled 'On the Influence of Physical Causes on Languages, Mythology, etc.', which in the manner of William Wilde aims to develop a 'geography of sounds' by examining the way language is affected by different physical terrains. The voice in mountainous regions is more modulated than on the plains, while pronunciation in cities is sharper, with an upward inflection of the vowels. (Sullivan's native Cork may have influenced this view.) As a kind of materialist, he is fascinated by the relations between the physical and natural sciences on the one hand, and language and culture on the other. In empiricist fashion, he is concerned with 'the influence of the sensual on the ideal',[79] in contrast with the inverse relation favoured by Ascendancy conservatives like Hamilton and de Vere. Sullivan also contributed an essay to a nationalist history of Ireland.[80] He was one of the mightiest, most versatile figures of Irish intellectual life, and an adequate intellectual biography of him is long overdue.

4

The Dismal Science

One of the most distinctive nineteenth-century Irish contributions to intellectual life came in the field of political economy. This was hardly surprising in a society where issues of rent, tenure, land ownership and the like were of such supreme importance. Economics is a good deal closer to the world of public affairs than ancient history or aesthetics, thus providing yet another opportunity for the intellectual to bridge the gap between academia and political society. Indeed, it was this very intimacy with the workaday world which cast doubt on political economy's credentials as a bona fide academic pursuit. It was not quite a vocation for gentlemen: Samuel Ferguson's execrable poem 'Inheritor and Economist' casts its Economist as a low-bred English *laissez-faire* fanatic, in contrast with the genteel cultivation of its Inheritor. Like medicine, political economy in Ireland could hardly avoid pointing beyond itself to social and political questions of broader import, where the 'generalist' Irish intellectual could once more find a home.

Political economy at the time found itself caught in a dilemma. To qualify as an authentic intellectual practice, it needed to insist on its independence of the material world; yet no discourse could be more palpably mundane. Some of its practitioners, in other words, tried to claim for themselves 'traditional' status, while being flagrantly 'organic'. If they established their science as truly disinterested, and so fit for academia, they were open to accusations of cold-hearted indifference in a field where human lives as well as livelihoods were potentially at stake. Yet if they acknowledged the eminently practical implications of their discipline, they were at risk of being no more than the mouthpieces of the merchant and the manufacturer.

What characterizes the Irish branch of the subject in the nineteenth century is its refusal to deny the inevitable utility of its findings. There are, as we shall see, exceptions to this rule; but in general Irish political economy, given the economic crisis raging about its ears, was prepared to trade scholarly disinterestedness and claims of universal validity for concrete humanistic ends. It was this, above all, which shaped its quarrel with its English counterparts. The universal abstractions of English Enlightenment thus found themselves at odds with the historical, political bent of Irish thought. William Thompson, perhaps the greatest radical thinker of nineteenth-century Ireland, formulates the conflict with gentle sarcasm:

> The *intellectual* speculators [on political economy], informed by their own feelings of the gentle, ever-springing and all-sufficient pleasures of sympathy and intellectual culture, their animal wants being all comfortably supplied and therefore exciting little of their attention, little studies [*sic*] perhaps of the physical laws of nature, of the physical constitution of man and the beings that surround him, conscious of their own powers of restraining and regulating what they regard as the grosser propensities of our nature, proclaim man as capable of attaining happiness by his mental powers alone, *almost* independent of material subordinate agency.[1]

Thompson's early, latently pejorative use of 'intellectual' to mean philosophically idealist is striking. His response to these high-minded moralists is to subject them to a materialist analysis, linking their idealism to their privileged status. The social conditions of their thought is thus made to contradict its actual claims. Thompson's own aim is 'to lead forth from the calm closets of philosophical inquiry, where they have delighted and elevated the minds of a *few*, into the world of life and action, those important truths [of political economy]'.[2] He is thus out to worst the traditional intellectuals by puncturing their otherworldliness; but if he rejects those political economists who 'wish to make man *all thought*' and 'affect to disdain *labour* as mechanical and grovelling',[3] he is equally severe on the mechanical materialists who overlook the intellect and reduce the human to the animal. Political economy must avoid the twin errors of severing itself from social interests and of being nothing but a reflex of them. And these, one might claim, are the respective temptations of the traditional and the organic intellectual. Thompson himself, who formulates in this work a theory of alienation – 'abstraction', as he calls it – which predates Marx's own, is convinced that if the laws of political economy are at loggerheads with those of universal morality, the former must bow to the latter. In this, he sounds a note which was to resound throughout the subsequent history of the subject in Ireland.

Indeed, what distinguishes the so-called Dublin school of nineteenth-century political economy is its generous-spirited humanism, its refusal to abstract economic matters from questions of general human welfare. Its English counterparts are in some ways more Mill, Ruskin and Morris than Smith, Ricardo and Bagehot.[4] In a judicious critique of English political economy, William Dillon complains that it 'has been elaborated and expounded almost exclusively by theorisers – men who have taken no active part in the practical management of the matters that form the subject of their teaching'. He can sympathize, he goes on, with the English political economists' 'horror of amateur criticism', but even so there is much to be said for such amateurism. On political economy, he considers, there are two equally inadequate schools of thought: those who would deny the title of 'higher knowledge' to any science which deals so directly with the material world, and those like John Elliott Cairnes who grant the subject that august status but deny its practical utility.[5] The traditional intellectual, in short, can either dismiss the subject out of hand, or claim it for his own camp by disowning its practical consequences. Dillon's is the voice of the Irish humanist speaking out against the disdain for practical reason of the traditional intellectual; it is also a smack at academic specialism in a society where a disinterested economics is plainly a myth. Political economy cannot help taking on the colour of its cultural environment; Adam Smith, Dillon sardonically observes, wrote a book on *The Wealth of Nations* which proceeds as though nations had no existence. Smith's abstractly universalizing logic simply ignores the reality of uneven national development, the inequalities between different civilizations and industrial states. To write from an underdeveloped colony is thus to question political economy's universalist claims.

One such Irish generalist who delved into economic affairs was Isaac Butt, lawyer, novelist, leader of the Irish parliamentary party, man-about-Dublin and pamphleteer on a range of topics from education and political federalism to church disestablishment and deep sea fisheries.[6] Carlyle described him as a 'terrible black burly son of earth . . . big bison-head, black, not *quite* unbrutal'.[7] He sees him as a Caribbean slave rather than an Anglo-Irish gentleman, and had an equal contempt for both. Despite holding a chair of political economy at Trinity, Butt was scarcely what we might now call a professional political economist, any more than the early occupants of chairs of English were professional literary critics or scholars. It would not occur to Butt, for example, to isolate economic issues from social and political ones. Indeed, given the condition of agrarian Ireland, it is hard to see how this would be possible. If his work on the land question in this sense predates the emergence of a professionalized political economy, it also prefigures a later, more 'totalizing' vein of social inquiry. Butt's 'moral' brand of political economy reflects the so-called moral economy of Irish society itself, where, in characteristic pre-modern fashion, some abstract paradigm of the economic is yet to be wholly disentangled from history, culture and custom. A unity of discourses thus reflects a specific social condition.[8]

What initially spurs Butt into 'economic' discourse is the politics of the Famine, as he lambasts the Whig relief policy of *laissez-faire*: 'If England had occasion to send an army into some country destitute of food, would her statesmen content themselves with seeing that the soldiers were regularly provided with their pay, and trust to the speculations of private enterprise to follow them with the necessary articles of food?'[9] The whole system of private property in Ireland 'is regarded by the great mass of the people as an alien institution, all its rights are looked upon as a force by conquest, and maintained only by a foreign force'.[10] It is standard nationalist rhetoric, which overlooks among other things a culture of deference among the tenantry; he is wrong, too, to claim elsewhere that the Irish tenants are 'serfs' or 'slaves', and to attribute an 'absolute power' to the landowners.[11] In any case, Butt himself has little to offer but the endlessly repeated panacea of fixity of tenure, as though a spreading of the so-called Ulster custom would stitch up the entire situation. But it was not, perhaps, quite so standard rhetoric for its time: Philip Bull argues that Butt 'lifted the debate about land tenure out of a context in which it had been reduced to a system which would remain basically unchanged', and finds in his agrarian writings 'the parameters of a new discourse on the land'. It is with Butt, Bull considers, that the land question is highlighted not only for its inherent importance, but 'as a symbol and token of a distinctive Irish identity'.[12]

In typical progressive-Unionist style, Butt's assessment of the landlord class is thoroughly ambivalent. It is also, perhaps, the ambivalence felt by the Anglo-Irish bourgeois towards the Anglo-Irish nobility. He is hot in defence of the gentry for their sterling work during the Famine, and exculpates them from callousness to the poor; but he also remarks of them in another context that

in no part of the country, except in some districts of Ulster, have they ever gathered round them a sympathising colony. The old instincts and traditions of the country have been too strong for them. In the midst of the nation, and yet scarcely of the nation, they stand in their possessions, isolated and alone. The habits, the modes of thought, the traditions, the religious observances of the two classes are all derived from distinct and even opposing origins. Real sympathy between the proprietors and the occupiers there is none.[13]

Yet it is this dismally unpromising material that the Young Turks of the *Dublin University Review*, spearheaded by Butt himself, hope to remodel into a spirited national leadership.

Like many of his Anglo-Irish intellectual colleagues, Butt – a writer of fiction himself, and a Romantic to the core – gives considerable emphasis to culture; yet it is precisely this which he sees as fissuring the nation, and thus threatening to shipwreck his political schemes of class-harmony. The Famine is as much an ethnic and cultural catastrophe as a social or economic disaster: 'Let no man see in the roofless walls of demolished habitations evidence of the "prosperity" which consists in consolidating a number of small farms into one great farm. These things constitute the ruin of the old nation – the nation that did not consist in the fields, and plains, and physical divisions of the country, but in the race of men who lived and moved on the soil. That race is going away'.[14] The cold-eyed view of progress here is among other things a gibe at English political economy from a humanistic 'economist' quite alien to that professional orthodoxy. In his sensitivity to custom and sentiment, Butt is a minor latter-day Burke, tugged between his political conciliationism and his moral fury. *The Irish People and the Irish Land* is a major work in that honourable lineage. 'I am not', Butt announces there, 'one of those who believe that grievances which may be called "sentimental" are therefore no grievances at all'.[15] Against the orthodox political economists, he recognizes that culture is as real as commodity production, that a science of society cannot simply 'bracket' subjectivity; but this appeal to traditional habits of feeling is also a conservative one. It is the Romantic Anglo-Irish intellectual, not the anaemic English utilitarian, who can read the hearts of the Irish people, and so can hope to unite them beneath his rule.

....

Not all contributors to political economy in Ireland shared Butt's capacious humanism. The English Whig cleric Richard Whately, who was to become Archbishop of Dublin in 1831, held the Drummond chair of political economy at Oxford, and hoped by doing so to give this still academically dubious discipline the seal of theological, perhaps even divine, approval. But his lectures on political economy firmly distinguish between economic and other matters, against the grain of Irish political economy in general. Man is defined, somewhat narrowly for some tastes, as 'an animal that makes *Exchanges*', and Whately notes with barely concealed satisfaction that even those other animals which approach our own

104

rationality seem to have no notion of bartering. Political economy as a field must be isolated, limited and severely defined.[16] As Lecky remarks of him, 'few considerable writers have appealed less to common passions or wide sympathies; and the only passion – if it can be called so – that appears strongly in his work, is the love of truth for its own sake, which is the rarest and highest of all'. Whately, in brief, is a pure instance of the traditional intellectual, dissevering knowledge from the public sphere.[17] Economic truths are one thing and moral or religious ones another, so that the purely technical discipline of political economy must refrain from moral judgements on whether, for example, wealth is good or bad. Having placed an embargo upon moral judgements, Whately then instantly proceeds to deliver a few of his own: the poor, he reminds us, can be just as vice-ridden as the rich, and 'luxury' is a relative term.

In the manner of patrician thinkers, Whately is a critic of empiricism, and deftly employs this critique of common sense to rebut the philistines for whom political economy means less a theory than the hard-headed business of making money. He recognizes that no observation can be value-free: no patient or nurse, he points out, could ever give a description of an illness that was innocent of theory and instead merely captured in neutral terms what was sensibly present to them. He sees too, with considerable shrewdness, that theory on a large scale is necessary only when social practices come unstuck: political economy is needed only when free exchange becomes clogged, rather as medical science arises to deal with the dysfunctional body. Having sharply separated economic and theological affairs, however, he then proceeds to reunite them. It is in the interests of the class he represents to define economic life as purely amoral, but also to lend it metaphysical backing, and Whately is caught helplessly in the contradiction. Divine wisdom guides the progress of human society, and private interest, like animal instinct, plays its ordained part in this magnificent cosmic design. Capitalism, in short, can be laid at the throne of the Almighty; and imperialism is justified because those in a 'savage state' cannot free themselves from it unassisted.[18] Colonialism thus turns out to be a disguised form of emancipation.

Whately's views were not on the whole shared by the greatest of

Irish economists of the day, John Elliott Cairnes, despite his occupation of the Whately chair of political economy at Trinity.[19] Whereas Whately wants to keep political economy clear of ethics but coupled to metaphysics, Cairnes desires just the opposite. On the one hand, he argues against expanding the category of political economy to include everything which affects the well-being of society; the subject should also keep its distance from philosophical speculation, as well as from practical policy. But for Cairnes there are no purely economic questions, since matters of public morality always intrude. This does not land him in the camp of the Positivists, for whom the notion of an autonomous political science is an illusion; economics, politics and morality form for Auguste Comte a unified ensemble. As a professional political economist out to defend the integrity of his discipline, Cairnes rejects this view; but he agrees with the need to contextualize the economic, and argues, in a style more acceptable to the Comteans, that we never encounter a purely economic, political or religious human being.[20] In Althusserian idiom, political economy is for him only a *relatively* autonomous pursuit, and social life is always over-determined. The science must not be narrowly identified with trade and finance, which has helped to discredit it in the eyes of some; it is part of a liberal education and an essential auxiliary to the study of history, since the laws of the development of wealth count among the most important influences on human conduct, and most men and women, after all, have spent their lives in toil. The laws of wealth are the key to the history of nations, though not the only one.

Cairnes thus lends his discipline foundational status, while scrupulously avoiding reductionism. If the historian is not also an economist, he simply recounts narratives without conceptual explanation. But he also rejects the over-valuing of his subject, which for him, in a Weberian distinction, has nothing to say of moral ends. Political economy is not the sole umpire in all social or political questions; it proposes truths rather than issues ethical commands, and a Kantian division between fact and value, theoretical and practical reason, is thus firmly instated. Cairnes thus manages to expand the empire of political economy with one hand while contracting it with the other. If the domain of morality is to remain autonomous,

106

one can either, *à la* Cairnes, define political economy narrowly enough to exclude it, or, in the manner of John Ruskin or John Kells Ingram, broaden the scope of ethics to include economics too.[21]

For Cairnes, the science of political economy encompasses both physical and mental laws, hovering at some indeterminate point in between them. Wealth is neither purely material nor wholly mental, but rather, as for John Ruskin, a complex composite of both. It is concerned neither just with the physical composition of the soil, nor with the peasant's feeling of self-interest, though both issues fall within its purview. It is 'the science of wealth, and of human well-being so far as this is dependent on wealth',[22] a definition which allows him to be both exact and broad-ranging. And human well-being differs from nation to nation. Since political economy deals with needs and desires along with more quantifiable matters, and since such desires are 'almost infinite', it will always be an uncertain science. There are, to be sure, certain stable psychological laws, such as the desire for wealth, an aversion to labour, a love of ease and immediate enjoyment; the ultimate truths of political economy, unlike those of some natural sciences, are directly present to our senses, and in this sense apodictic. But these general, *a priori* laws are always culturally modified, cropping up in different guises from one society to another. Patriotism, for example, with its appeal to buy only a certain national product, is one such modification of their force. The laws of gravity, Cairnes points out, are similarly qualified by the action of friction. In any case, these laws are more hypothetical tendencies than absolute realities, and always carry with them some *ceteris paribus* clause.[23]

Cairnes's thought, like that of his friend John Stuart Mill, is thus suspended somewhere between naturalism and historicism. Political economy is not to be reduced to a science of naked, unhistorical Economic Man, or to some absolutely invariant human psychology, but neither is it to be historicized away. Adam Smith, Cairnes approvingly comments, appeals to history without ever making it the basis of his economic doctrine.[24] He himself remains a deductivist of that school: whatever the fluctuations of circumstance, certain psychological principles remain unvarying. Even so, he wrote a brief essay on 'Imaginary Geometry and the Truth of Axioms' which endorses the mathematician Helmholtz's opinion that not even geometrical truths are universal or absolute; they would not be so, for example, for beings who inhabited four-dimensional space.

It is this aversion to an unqualified naturalism, with its latently determinist tendencies, which leads Cairnes to dissent from the sociology of Herbert Spencer. Against Spencer's determinism, he highlights a diversity of culture and character; *pace* Spencer's belief that the individual units of social life determine the whole, he argues that the units themselves can behave unpredictably as they enter into mutually transformative relation with one another. The elements of society are polyvalent, and do not necessarily 'determine its structure to a particular form'.[25] Spencer tends to assume fatalistically that the social structure is fixed, overlooking this free play or dialectic between part and whole; Cairnes, as an enlightened reformist, finds this view 'philosophically unsound and practically mischievous',[26] since it reifies the present state of society and deprives us of political hope. He himself believes in the possibility of social engineering, offering as a fruitful example the Irish Tithe Commutation Act. Though he approves in orthodox Victorian fashion of Spencer's attempt to place the study of society on a soundly scientific basis, he finds his homology between the social and the individual organism highly speculative. It is also, he thinks, a logically flawed analogy, since individual organisms are affected by forces external to them, whereas it is hard to imagine what would count as the 'outside' of society. 'Another society' would clearly be no answer. In Positivist style, Spencer illicitly transposes physiological and zoological laws to history and culture, whereas Cairnes, as a partial 'culturalist' or historicist, wants to resist this Comtean reductionism.

It is a reductionism which in the case of both Comte and Spencer goes hand-in-hand with an untempered scientific progressivism, a dogma which Cairnes is also keen to rebut. As a colonial intellectual, standing somewhat to the side of the metropolitan intellectual establishment, he casts doubt on its hubristic ideology of linear, uninterrupted evolution. Ireland is hardly a good example of the beneficent workings of the laws of Nature. On the contrary, he argues, many nations have historically regressed (he cites Turkey as an example), while the Orient as a whole has remained stagnant and stationary. No single global law can be forced upon these markedly uneven societies; instead, different historical patterns must be distinguished. It is preposterous to model human society on the animal kingdom, since for one thing (unless one is a Lamarckian heretic) animal evolution does not come about by the conscious effort of those involved. Human evolution, by contrast, finally arrives at the stage where its agents are able to plan and redirect it through conscious, collective action, taking social goals as their individual ends. Cairne's social corporatism is more in line with the thought of Thomas Huxley than with Herbert Spencer, and its openness to social reform, as against Spencer's complacent triumphalism, reflects the attitudes of one reared in a society crying out for reconstruction. It also reflects a colony more accustomed than England to the idea of state intervention, as well as an intellectual caste who are themselves on the whole more 'statist' than their metropolitan counterparts.

Cairnes takes issue here with Spencer's fatalistic use of the word 'spontaneous' to describe social development. Why is private enterprise 'spontaneous', but state intervention somehow not? Cairnes's own humanist emphasis is on human agency, whereas Spencer holds in Comtean manner that since social improvement will come about anyway, thanks to the teleological thrust of natural laws, any attempt to bring it consciously about is at best superfluous and at worst actively harmful. But the metaphor underlying this opinion is in Cairne's view a falsifying one: the notion that societies grow in much the same way that plants do. It is a trope unlikely to impress one from a society which could hardly be said to be flourishing like an oak tree under its own innate impulses. Such a doctrine, as Cairnes recognizes, succeeds in abolishing the political, a move perhaps more plausible in London than in Belfast. For both Cairnes and Mill, the social depends upon the political in the sense that it is political forces which determine whether social evolution is upward or downward. And since political outcomes are always uncertain, this too strikes a blow at the belief in iron laws of history. Cairnes, to be sure, is unable unlike Mill to reconcile his trust in human agency with his quasi-determinist belief that every action is a link in a chain of motivations; as with Immanuel Kant, he simply accepts the reality of both spheres, without struggling to resolve them. But he is clear that Spencer's own case is logically self-cancelling, since his own action in preaching the gospel of social determinism is itself presumably determined. Thus either there is no need for it, or it can be dismissed as just another part of the process it describes rather than an illuminating comment upon it from outside.[27]

Cairnes's Burkean insistence on cultural specificities, a particularism which influenced Mill's progressive line on Ireland, has a root in his Irish experience.[28] As the century approached its close, with one Irish Land Act tumbling on the heels of another, it was becoming harder to overlook the contradiction between the laws of classical political economy and such Irish practices as the state regulation of contracts between landowners and tenants. As an Irish scholar in England, Cairnes could also register the cultural relativity of a supposedly timeless English political economy in a way less available to the insiders. He could also see just how the specific features of Irish society thrust it outside the English economic paradigm. The Englishman Sir George Campbell declared, in the spirit of John Stuart Mill, that 'as the world now stands, it is we who are abnormal, and the Irish system is that which is more general'.[29]

In a remarkably dignified, eloquent, lethal riposte to J. A. Froude's racist history of Ireland, Cairnes brands Froude a Carlylean absolutist who takes no regard of 'the traditions, customs, and general state of civilisation' of the society he is examining, and who in Positivist style fatally confuses human and physical laws.[30] Froude's book, he considers, bears about the same relation to actual history as a moralistic novel does to the highest order of fiction. He himself, he points out, is a Unionist, but Froude's history will simply rekindle nationalist passions at a critical time. His review is in an exact sense a deconstruction of the text, disclosing the way it unconsciously violates its own governing logic. Since Froude's justification for colonialism is self-declaredly pragmatic – only those who govern effectively have the right to rule, in a Carlylean might-is-right equation – then Froude's portrait of England's miserable misgovernment of Ireland has in fact undermined his own case. If English power failed in the colony, then by his own logic it should have with-

110

drawn, and the Irish had a right to rebel. The Irish are painted as the plundered victims of a scandalous sovereignty; then, when they rise up against rulers with no natural sanction to govern, they are shown up as louts and murderers. Irish disaffection, contradictorily, is both a natural consequence of misrule and an unprovoked treachery, and the Irish demand for political equality is treated by Froude as some peculiar abnormality in their nature.

In some later essays, Cairnes resumes his preoccupation with the fact/value question, which in the case of political economy can be recast as the relation between academic theory and political practice. Judging by the comparative numbers of students of the subject in London and Galway ('that remote, and I regret to say decaying, Irish town'), the Irish seem considerably more interested in the question than those in the very national birthplace of the discipline. Cairnes speculates that the pursuit may be unpopular in England because it appears no more than the codifying of the principles of *laissez-faire*, and has thus won itself a bad name as politically tendentious. In any case, if this principle has triumphed in society, why bother with the science of it at all? He himself, however, regards the principle of *laissez-faire* as having 'no scientific basis whatsoever': it is 'at best a mere handy rule of practice . . . totally destitute of all scientific authority'.[31] If Cairnes the compassionate social reformer speaks here, so does the intellectual reluctant to see his sovereignty usurped by the merchants and the clerks. Human interests, he believes, are basically at one, but class interests are not necessarily so. In any case, what people hold to be in their interests is culturally variable, and Cairnes has already grasped the modern doctrine that we are not in this respect self-transparent. Industrial freedom in Britain is greater than anywhere else, but so also is the gap between rich and poor, all of which casts doubt on the sanctity of *laissez-faire* philosophy. The metropolitan nation is characterized by pauperism, the elite ownership of land, an agricultural population washed up in workhouses and 'frightful commercial catastrophe' which regularly overtakes artisans. One man's meal could feed another's family for a month. 'We have', he declares, 'no sign of mitigation in the harshest features of our social state'[32] – though he adds that *laissez-faire*, for all its evils, is incomparably better than state control.

In the case of Ireland, however, Cairnes believes that the state must indeed play a role in regulating the business of land. Land cannot be treated as just another commodity, since social circumstances may confer on a product a higher value than the producer's labour would lend it. And Irish landlords must not be allowed to raise their rents at will. In framing such political judgements, however, Cairnes does not exactly see himself as speaking in the persona of the political economist. Political economy itself is absolutely neutral, with no more commitment to *laissez-faire* than to communism. It is as dispassionate in this respect as chemistry is to different schemes of sanitation. He thus manages to salvage the autonomy of his subject, in the manner of the traditional intellectual, while cannily detaching it from a defence of the status quo, which is rather less in the manner of the traditional intellectual. Political economy is not just the theoretical justification of our present way of life; it is not, in short, an ideology.[33] If he defends a Kantian distinction between fact and value, the descriptive and the normative, it is largely because he wants to resist the Leibnizian or Bolingbrokian doctrine that whatever is, is right. Ironically, then, Cairnes's devotion to value-free science carries with it some political implications unpalatable to some of those who would most endorse that disinterestedness.

It is not for nothing, then, that he is still best known in international circles as the author of *The Slave Power*, a passionate indictment of American slavery which had a deep influence on British public opinion and made him illustrious in his own time. (The other chief source of his celebrity was his writing on gold, which ranks among the most influential works of nineteenth-century monetary theory.) *The Slave Power* was a sharp, splendid intervention from the colonial margins on one of the most vital topics of the day.[34] It was written to counteract a certain British softness on the US southern states, revealing slavery to be both morally obnoxious and economically unviable. In the finest traditions of the 'Dublin school', it is a work of morality and political economy at the same time. It is also the work of an Irish scholar cutting against the English grain: the centrality of slavery in the American Civil War, he maintains elsewhere, is being evaded or palliated in England, where organs such as the *Saturday Review* can announce that the vast majority of American blacks 'have no grievances whatever except in the fact that they are slaves'.[35] Cairnes, by contrast, wants to recall Britain from 'its unnatural infatuation for a Slave Power' to its traditional role as 'the emancipator of slaves, the champion of the oppressed, and the friend of freedom in every form'.[36] It is not exactly clear which particular British championing of the oppressed Cairnes has in mind, but it is evident that he writes among other things as a colonial intellectual, impatient with British shuffling and foot-dragging on a question which he regards as 'the greatest curse which has darkened the earth'.[37] Darwin was deeply impressed by *The Slave Power*, while Marx based some of his own ideas about slavery on the study. He would no doubt have approvingly underlined Cairnes's assertion in the preface that 'the course of history is largely determined by the action of economic causes'. Irish economists found it hard to avoid a certain spontaneous materialism – partly because they were economists, and partly because of Ireland. This even applies to the far-from-materialist Lecky, who writes that 'few things contribute so much to the formation of the social type as the laws regulating the succession of property, and especially the agglomeration or division of landed property'.[38] Unwitting Marxism seems an occasional consequence of the prominence in Ireland of the property question.

Cairnes's opposition to colonialism was impressively emphatic for its time. On the whole, he looks benevolently on the actual history of colonial government; but it has now reached a point of crisis, passed its peak and come to outlive its usefulness. He divides colonial history into three phases: mercantilist colonialism, which he sees as driven by a thirst for precious metals; modern colonialism, in which this commercial motive is subordinate to problems of excess population and the need for new industrial outlets; and contemporary colonialism, where these rationales are becoming redundant, as colonies like Canada move towards what he sees as an entirely reasonable independence. As an opponent of Home Rule, he does not extend this tolerance to Ireland, perhaps because he does not regard it as a colony in the first place. The British empire has now reached its natural goal, but this will not diminish Britain's power and influence in the future. It will instead take the form of a new kind of 'moral community', bound by ties of blood, language, law, literature and religion rather than by the dictats of the Colonial Office. One may thus add to the roll-call of Cairnes's other achievements a striking anticipation of the Commonwealth.[39]

Political economy was not in Cairnes's view a stable science. Since everything which affects human character and institutions threw up fresh problems for it, its object was constantly changing. He believed, for example, that the growth of the cooperative movement had thrown the discipline into a certain disarray, since a body of theory so firmly centred on the distinction between labourer and capitalist found it hard to elucidate a project in which, as in peasant proprietorship, these roles were identified. Cairnes opposed socialism, which he regarded as a 'rank outgrowth of economic ignorance';[40] if political economy was scientifically neutral, its even-handedness did not quite extend to the Paris Commune, which for Cairnes represented a 'terrible catastrophe'. Yet he believed that rent should be controlled by law rather than market forces, and startled Irish public opinion by promoting peasant proprietorship as early as 1865. He could also well understand why the working class was repelled by his own discipline, given its notorious identification with *laissez-faire*. J. M. Keynes considered Cairnes 'perhaps the first orthodox economist to deliver a frontal attack upon *laissez faire* in general'.[41] There were those, Cairnes remarked, who 'have their own reasons for not cherishing that unbounded admiration for our present industrial arrangements'[42] which political economists tend to evince, and his sympathy with them was to some extent bound up with his Irishness. He writes of Ireland's 'wretched peasantry, demoralised by centuries of industrial insecurity',[43] and this fellow-feeling with the Irish tenantry extends to the English working class too. It is not surprising that they should be so wary of political economy, he remarks, when they see it condemning strikes and cooperatives but approving of capital accumulation.

Even so, the Unionist Cairnes was certainly no historical materialist, and in his *Leading Principles of Political Economy* explicitly rejects the Marxist slogan of giving to each according to his needs. The use of state power in this area can mean only 'disaster and ruin'. Though trade unions have a limited role, he is sceptical of their ability to affect the law of wages. But there is no reason either to assume with the French economist Bastiat and his ilk that the economic status quo is a just one; indeed, it is hard, Cairnes considers, to reconcile the practical consequences of industry with 'any standard of right generally accepted among men'.[44] Mill, he thinks, has disposed of communism, and private self-interest, though a 'coarse' motivation, has proved efficacious as altruism and benevolence would not. But private property is nevertheless far from fixed and absolute. The only balm for the 'harsh and hopeless destiny' of the working class is for them to limit their numbers (a move which Cairnes illiberally believes should be enforced), and to scramble out of the proletariat to become capital investors themselves. The phenomenal amount they currently spend on alcohol must be saved and invested in cooperatives, though these would by no means replace private property. Cairnes compares such cooperatives to tenant proprietorship in Ireland, and claims that they would discipline and morally elevate the working class. To rise from their dependency on capital is the only hope for the labourers. Capitalist 'progress', he observes with harsh realism, has not benefited the mass of workers, and will not do so; one can expect social inequalities to grow. In this bleak vision, he is far from the progressivist optimism of a Comte or a Spencer.

Cairnes was a liberal figure of public importance, hostile to a Catholic hierarchy who, so he thought, wanted to charter the Catholic University not as a supplement to the Queen's colleges but as a sectarian alternative to them. The church under Cullen has become Roman, not Irish, in spirit. He defends the colleges as potential antidotes to bigotry, a neutral ground on which different denominations may meet and learn mutual respect. In Newmanite terms, he sees the purpose of a university as the 'largest and freest development in all directions of the national mind'.[45] Unlike Newman, however, he develops what might be called a materialist theory of knowledge, one which leads him all the way from the immediate needs of the body to the higher learning. The body knows instinctively its material needs, and acts to satisfy them; but our mental needs are less easy to determine, and here we need the intervention of the state in order to educate us. Since the desire for knowledge only arises from having some knowledge already, those who lack it are in need of state guidance. In a subsequent stage, however, knowledge accrues a 'marketable value', so that state supports may fall away. But when we come to the higher knowledges like science and philosophy, which can never find a market value, the state once more becomes essential in the form of the universities.

The role of such academies is to foster these apparently useless, non-profitable forms of knowledge, just as the state needs to support those who are too ignorant to desire knowledge or too poor to acquire it. The end of the university, Cairnes quotes Mill as observing, is to 'keep philosophy alive', and so to stand askew to the market place. Truth is its own reward; but it is also useful in the sense of furnishing us with the ethical and political principles on which to base our conduct. The distinction between practical and useless knowledge is to that extent dismantled, as truth becomes a practical affair at the higher end of this process just as it was at its lowly material beginning. The task of the universities, Cairnes declares in a fine flourish in his inaugural lecture at University College Galway, is to prevent 'our arts from degenerating into empiricism, our trades into mysteries, and our professions into the impudent pretensions of the quack'.[46] 'Many unworthy acts have been committed in the name of Liberty; but we question if the sacred word was ever more audaciously prostituted than when invoked by ultramontane bishops against the system of education established by Sir Robert Peel'.[47]

As an advocate of civic rights, as well as an economist, educationalist and philosopher, Cairnes stands in an honourable lineage of Irish intellectual humanists. If he belongs to a newly professionalized academia, defending the scientific status of his subject against accusations of amateurism and ideology, he also participates in the public sphere of the man of letters. Indeed, much of his work, and not least his humanistic view of political economy, is moulded by one of England's most pre-eminent men of letters, John Stuart Mill, who drew a good deal from Cairnes for his own writings on Ireland.[48] His humane, reformist politics, a combination of populist sympathies and capitalist priorities, represent the best of the liberal Unionist heritage.[49]

....

Despite his progressive views, Cairnes has been dubbed ' the most orthodox of all classical economists'.[50] Theoretically speaking he was a Ricardian, while the first four professors to hold the Whately chair – Longfield, Butt, Lawson and Hancock – moved away from this orthodox, cost-of-production theory of prices to more subjective notions of them. In fact the Dublin school of political economy was noted for this subjectivist challenge to English economic orthodoxy.[51] Mountiford Longfield, a lawyer and the first holder of the Whately chair, seeks in his *Four Lectures on Poor Laws* to rebut the case that political economy is hard-hearted, and claims that it is out to ameliorate the conditions of the poor. This, however, does not prevent him from arguing for a strictly limited poor law which would be severe on the able-bodied, since 'it is impossible to raise the pauper without depressing the labourer'.[52] But he is generous to the old and disabled, for whom he demands an annual pension, and declares that every individual is entitled to support from the state. Indeed, he has been hailed as an early precursor of the modern welfare state.[53] Ironically, the social and economic backwardness of Ireland, which required some strenuous state intervention, prefigured modern times more than did the more advanced social order of Victorian England.

A more full-blooded historicist than Cairnes was Thomas Edward Cliffe Leslie, who like Richard Whately was an anti-essentialist when it comes to the definition of wealth. The love of money, he argues, is not to be moralistically denounced, since it really means the love of a vast number of different things of which money is the mere medium. Wealth is multiple, and so also are the laws of evolution of different forms of wealth and their particular cultural institutions. All this is concealed by the philosophical realism of English economists of the Ricardian school, who falsely homogenize this plurality under a single abstract noun. Cliffe Leslie, for his part, is rather more nominalist about the matter: love of money includes the desire for knowledge, health, decency, peace, culture and liberty. In typically 'Dublin' style, he thus 'socializes' the narrowly economic conception of wealth, unpacking its cultural implications. He defends Adam Smith, whose founding principle he believes to be not selfishness but liberty, and considers Cairnes to be the leading economist of the day, strongly supporting his anti-slavery campaign. In Cairnes's own historicist, particularizing fashion, he sees political economy not as 'a body of natural truths' but 'an assemblage of speculations and doctrines which are the result of a particular history'.[54] This perhaps presses his colleague's own historicism a little further than he himself would wish to travel. All of our moral and philosophical doctrines would look different if history had happened otherwise. Smith failed to recognize this in Cliffe Leslie's view, though he sees his work as a blend of the historical and the rational-deductive, unifying these approaches by the doctrine that the empirical or historical investigation of Nature disclosed certain abiding *a priori* laws. Indeed, he historicizes Smith himself, relating his work to a less developed stage of Scottish industrial production in which the notion of natural laws might appear more plausible. Had Smith lived two generations later, he would have written differently.

Cliffe Leslie admires the 'consummate literary art' of Cairnes's *Leading Principles of Political Economy*, though Cairnes is too close to the English non-historicist school for his own taste, and he dissents from much in his findings and methodology. His *Slave Power*, however, he regards as one of the most masterly essays ever to have graced the history of the subject. It is largely due to Cairnes, Cliffe Leslie declares, that the Irish universities are not under ultramontane control. As an enthusiast for the German school of historical and philosophical political economy, he is much more of a social totalizer than Cairnes, and much closer to John Kells Ingram: political economy is locked into a general science of society. Mill is too concerned with production, and Whately with exchange, whereas Cliffe Leslie himself wants to examine the more variable conditions of consumption, and in Positivist fashion refuses any final distinction between the economic and the rest of social life. Economic forces, he writes, 'are not only connected, but identical, with forces which are also moral and intellectual . . . our whole national economy is a historical structure. . . . How long a history lies behind the feelings with which the land is regarded, and its price in the market, as well as behind its existing distribution!'[55] The pure milk of the economic is a rarer commodity in Ireland than in England, given the close meshing in the colony of property and custom, prices and social practice. The 'Dublin' economists, writing in a society more backward and traditional than Britain, have not yet reached the point where an abstraction called the 'economic' can be extracted whole and entire from the complexities of cultural history. The clash between them and the English school is thus a result of the non-synchronic histories of the two islands. But this Irish 'backwardness' is also a kind of progressivism, as the Dublin school is well aware: it is the political left who will insist that the 'economic' is always enmeshed in specific social relations.

Cliffe Leslie thus refuses the naturalistic assumption, one strongly at work in both Mill and Cairnes, that there is a phenomenon called 'love of gain' which is somehow foundational. 'Conjugal and parental affection', for example, are for him the most powerful forces influencing production and consumption, but the family, so he maintains, has figured as a mere blank in classical political economy. The small Irish farm lies somewhere beneath his economic thought, as the industrial factory lurks beneath that of his English counterparts. The poor man's wife, he claims, is the hardest worked of all labourers. It is hardly a familiar note in nineteenth-century political economy. The economist, he insists, 'must penetrate even into the most romantic passions and sentiments of the human heart',[56] mindful of the fact that without sentimental marriages, house-builders, clergymen and lawyers would be impoverished.[57] In any case, desires are culturally variable: if the French desire property, the English hanker for beer. Wants and ends arise from historical communities, not from natural propensities. Cultural forms actively transform economic forces – he supplies the quaint example of the influence of French duelling on pistol production – and there is no law of natural indolence. Economic reductionism simply neglects such phenomena as the massive importance of warfare in the middle ages, as well as the importance of religion, the family, love and morality in social life.

As civilization develops, so in Cliffe Leslie's view does a love of exertion for its own sake, and employment becomes essential for happiness. The appetitive human being of classical political economy is a fiction, and he quotes with relish Walter Bagehot's dictum that English political economy applies only to English males of the present day. The discipline's myopic concern with the individual ignores

119

history and corporate agency, realities perhaps rather more palpable in the Ireland of the day. Its faith in scientific precision is equally misconceived: Cliffe Leslie's own epistemology takes account of the opaque, indeterminate nature of economic affairs, their shifting and elusive character. Knowledge does not have to be absolute and unequivocal in order to be scientific. Classical political economy posits a world of light, order, equality and perfect organization, in contrast to the confusion, waste, obscurity and happenstance we actually have. It 'leads men to imagine an unreal uniformity and order in the world, corresponding with their own classifications'.[58] Like Cairnes, he is sceptical of Herbert Spencer's law of increasing heterogeneity: it is not true, for example, of languages, which begin as diffuse and then grow more uniform and centralized.

The radicalism of Cliffe Leslie's work, in a postmodern age which like him values plurality, indeterminacy, historicism, anti-essentialism, the centrality of culture and sexuality and the 'constructed' nature of desire, has gone strangely unsung. He is far ahead of his time, and in some ways strikingly original. He also has the additional virtue of being for the most part right. But his radicalism is not simply theoretical. In his work *Land Systems and Industrial Economy*, which treats of Germany, Belgium, England and Ireland, he asserts that 'the man does not exist who could give a complete and true account of Ireland's present condition'.[59] Why has the English land system failed in Ireland? Cliffe Leslie's tart reply is because it has not worked in England either. Like Cairnes, he is a keen proponent of tenant proprietorship, and makes short work of the myth that it is mainly lower-class violence which keeps capital investment out of Ireland. The history of Ireland has been 'one long profligate waste of natural resources', and the Irish landlords 'are the creatures of a violent interference with pre-existing rights of property'.[60] Like that of most of his caste, however, Cliffe Leslie's radicalism has its stringent limits. As an anti-separatist and anti-Fenian, as well as something of an Anglophile, he seeks a closer union with Britain, which will help Ireland to shake off the 'torpor of ages'. If he speaks of the wretchedness of the colony, he also praises the glories of the metropolis.

....

120

The political economist John Kells Ingram has been remembered on the whole only for his youthful verse 'The Memory of the Dead', with its rousing opening line 'Who fears to speak of Ninety-Eight?' One answer to the query might well be 'John Kells Ingram', who spent much of the rest of his cloistered career trying to live it down. Born in Donegal but educated like John Mitchel in Newry, Ingram became president of the Royal Irish Academy and vice-provost of Trinity College, where he produced a formidable body of work. Thomas Carlyle describes him approvingly as 'wholly English (that is to say, Irish-rational) in sentiment'.[61] 'Irish-rational' denotes for Carlyle a very select company indeed. As a 'public' intellectual as well as a Trinity don, he played a central role in the work of the Statistical Society of Dublin, founded in 1847 under the influence of the Famine. Butt, Whately, Kane, Wilde and Ferguson were also involved in the Society's work. He was also a fine geometrician, and wrote on Shakespeare; Tyrrell praised him as 'probably the best educated man in the world'.[62] He was also one of the very few Irish intellectuals to espouse the creed of Positivism,[63] made a pilgrimage to the home of Auguste Comte and seems to have practised some of the rather more arcane rituals of the Religion of Humanity. In his *Practical Morals*, he looks forward to a worldwide corporation, presided over by the High-Priest of Humanity, equipped with 'sacerdotal' schools, social sacraments and the rest of the Comtean paraphernalia.[64] Comte's doctrine, with its stress on the inseparability of the social, political and economic, suited the humanist bias of Dublin political economy, though his epistemological assurance and relentless historical progressivism was, as we have seen, rather less well-adapted to the condition of Ireland as a whole. Like Comte, Ingram believed in the social perfectibility of humanity, a heroic act of faith in nineteenth-century Ireland.

In his *History of Political Economy*, Ingram proposes a humane version of the dismal science as a study of *mentalities*, more a part of the history of consciousness than of the history of production. This, too, consorts well with the subjectivist bias of the Dublin school. Like Cliffe Leslie, he is resolutely hostile to the English school's abstraction of political economy from the totality of social existence. He counters this English abstraction rather craftily by providing a historical account of the rise and fall of economic theories them-selves, thus historicizing a phenomenon whose central tenets claim to be immune from historical influence. His book, so to speak, is a study of economic *Geist*, of those great Lecky-like currents of histori-cal consciousness of which particular individuals are merely the bearers. He is also coolly unabashed by the ethical relativism which flows from this historicism: ancient slavery was probably a 'tempo-rary necessity' and even a 'relative good'.[65] (Elsewhere, Ingram is rather less restrained in his approval of slavery, which in his *History of Slavery and Serfdom* has become an 'immense advance' on barba-rism, and at least made for standards of industriousness.[66]) Positiv-ism, with its concern with corporate life and historical evolution, has now overtaken the ahistorical egoism of classical political economy, with its timeless dogmas of 'national selfishness and pri-vate cupidity'.[67] He commends Montesquieu for having discovered the natural laws of social development, and in triumphalist Comtean fashion sees economic history – largely deterministic if sometimes morally deplorable – as culminating in the 'synthesis' of his own time.

The synthesis in question is among other things one between general laws and specific phenomena. With his Positivist zeal for the observation of social facts, Ingram admires what he sees as Adam Smith's empirical rather than rationalist approach to political economy; but it is now time to re-order these facts according to general laws, which will be of the historical-inductive rather than rational-deductive kind. Smith's work still retains the trace of meta-physical concepts such as natural rights, but anticipates the Comtean synthesis in its Scottish Enlightenment sensitivity to the historical spirit. His negative, critical project was essential but insufficient: it remains too individualist, too anti-interventionist, and by no means moral enough. Smith fails to grasp that wealth is a means to the higher ends of life, or to recognize that stages of economic develop-ment correspond to different phases of social evolution. His work must itself be set in historical context: it predates the full flourishing of industrial society, the more deplorable effects of which might well have tempered Smith's rather too sanguine outlook.

Mill, however, is acclaimed for his refusal to treat economics in isolation from society, though the influence of Comte on his work has not penetrated deeply enough. He also 'entertained strongly exaggerated, or rather perverted, notions of the "subjection", the capacities, and the rights of women'.[68] Feminism was hardly Positivism's strongest point. In a related lapse of rectitude, Mill also encouraged the spirit of revolt in 'men', by which Ingram means in effect the working class. Cairnes, who held too rigorously to the deductivist method, is methodologically unsound: as a traditionalist devotee of Smith and Ricardo, he predates the 'Historical School' (Ingram's code for Comtism) and has been superannuated along with the rest of classical political economy.[69] Cliffe Leslie, by contrast, is extolled as producing the first systematic statement in English of the historical method.

Ingram's programme, both epistemologically and politically, is tenaciously Positivist. Political economy must be wrested from the grip of the 'lawyers and men of letters', purged of its theologico-metaphysical residues of rights, natural liberty, teleology, optimism and the like, and transformed into part of a bona fide social science. The genteel-amateur humanists, in short, are now yielding ground to the hard-nosed academic professionals – though Ingram's Positivism preserves, ironically, the generous scope of the genteel amateurs in its synoptic view of society. It is simply that this must now be raised to the level of scientific reputability,[70] rather than left in the bungling hands of the men of letters, divines like Whately or lawyers such as Butt and Longfield. Ingram's agenda, like Cairnes's, thus involves both an expansion and contraction of the field, scooping up political economy into historical sociology while jealously defending its scientific credentials. In this way, an ideal combination of 'generalist' intellectual and specialist academic can be achieved, the latter buttressed in his professional status but with no detriment to his right to pronounce on everything under the sun. A scientific political economy belongs to both sociology and morality, but since morality is itself an objective science, this is no contradiction.

Politically speaking, this synthetic science of society aims at class-synthesis too. Like his Parisian master, Ingram sets his face against both social revolution and *laissez-faire*, and like Comte considers that talk of rights – a metaphysical hangover from a revolutionary epoch – must now give way to talk of functions. What will redeem society – another Comtean cliché – is not so much legislation, though Ingram is a state interventionist, as the nurturing of profound convictions about social duties. Ironically, this briskly anti-metaphysical creed ends up as yet another form of commonplace idealism, for which, as for John Stuart Mill, it is education and public opinion which will save the day. Its solutions thus fall some way short of the way it has defined the problems.

In an address of 1880 to the Trade Union Congress in London, Ingram seized the rare opportunity of casting his Positivist notions into the public sphere. In Comtean style, he proposes a moral solution to industrial conflict. What is needed is a 'generally accepted code of social duties', which comes down to a socially responsible capitalism with a paternalist concern for its workers and a cult of the dignity of labour. Capitalists must conduct themselves like army officers or view themselves as 'social administrators'; in seeking to befriend their employees and ceasing to treat them as commodities, *richesse oblige* must become their slogan. This neo-feudalist panacea, advanced by one of the most self-consciously avant-garde currents of the age, is not altogether remote from the thought of Standish O'Grady. Master and worker fulfil different but equally essential roles, and the worker is a prime example of Comtean altruism, since he 'lives for others'. Whether the others in question are Comte's Humanity or the bosses is not made clear. Ingram approves of the corporate nature of trade unions, which fits well enough with the anti-individualist programme of his mentor, but disapproves of their devotion to their own material well-being, which does not. Tactfully, he omits to mention to the assembled delegates of labour his opposition to the extension of secondary education to the working class, a policy which would encourage 'vicious efforts to rise above [their] class'.[71]

If the intellectual is the medium through which ideas take on a political incarnation, Ingram can certainly be said to qualify for the title. Scientific accuracy, *pace* the traditional intellectual, is not just an end in itself: on the contrary, 'by establishing the laws which regulate social phenomena, it sobers and tranquillises the mind,

124

showing that the fundamental constitution of practical life is be-yond our control . . . and that no popular sovereignty, ever so unani-mous, can alter the essential nature of things'.[72] In a single bold swoop, Ingram can move from epistemological exactitude to the discrediting of radical politics. The end of sociology is to remind us of our utter powerlessness, so that the more we know, the less we can do. It is not clear whether it is the voice of sociology, or of Trinity, which speaks here. The sociologist has now become the chief organic intellectual of the industrial middle class, deploying his very specialism in the name of wider political ends, and conse-crating the market place with the chrism of science. But in case this fatalism should breed an ideologically dangerous gloom, Ingram instantly resounds the high-minded Victorian note: reform and 'hopeful effort' are always possible. It is a familiar Victorian combi-nation of glum determinism and dogged cheerfulness: by adapting to the laws which govern our behaviour, we can always hope to manipulate them to our advantage.

It is cheerfulness rather than gloom which marks Ingram's view of Ireland in 1864. Emigration he sees as a perfectly natural phe-nomenon, part of the great march of historical progress; indeed, the Irish positively want to emigrate, and lamenting this exodus would be like mourning the flow of the tides. It is a natural law that labour will gravitate to the highest wage, so that the Irish emigrants are merely the bearers of historical destiny. Unlike Cairnes and Cliffe Leslie, he wants to see the end of the small tenantry, who should be converted to farm labourers by the consolidation of the land. Britain thus provides the paradigm for agrarian society as a whole. Nine-teenth-century Ireland, from the Union to Emancipation and on-wards, bears witness to the reality of progress, though the Famine goes diplomatically unmentioned. What this upbeat narrative teaches is the truth that 'the governing classes of the empire are perfectly accessible to evidence and argument'.[73] Whether they are also ac-cessible to acting upon them is not examined.

Ingram was not himself wholly free of a touch of metaphysics. His *Human Nature and Morals According to Auguste Comte* identifies eight-een functions of the human brain, in which the affective faculties predominate over the intellectual ones. Politically speaking, this means that a change of heart takes precedence over a change of institutions. In a classic piece of Hobbesianism, he regards individuals as driven primarily by instinct, with intellect as a mere calculative instrument for promoting them. The last word in scientific progress is thus distinctly old-hat. The instincts include military and industrial drives, which Ingram, unlike Cliffe Leslie, accordingly naturalizes, and the aim of the Religion of Humanity is to inculcate altruism on a scale ascending from family to nation to humanity itself. An 'advanced', scientific psychology thus mysteriously turns out to underwrite traditional middle-class values. The seat of the maternal instinct, he considers, is 'above the cerebellum in the median part of the lower posterior brain',[74] though how he came by this sensational information remains unclear. The desire for power is located beside the industrial instinct, while 'Firmness (or Perseverance) is a median organ situated in the space formerly left vacant, behind Benevolence and in front of the Desire of Approbation'.[75] All this is dire testimony to the dangers of skulking too long in one's Trinity rooms. Human beings must come to devote themselves to the Great Being of Humanity, a creature whom Ingram, in one of his few gestures to women, reverently genders as female. The so-called selfish instincts are really elaborate psychological code for the proletariat – Ingram writes darkly of these instincts' 'sudden and unforeseen assaults' – while 'altruism' means taming and integrating these unruly drives by the governance of middle-class administrators, bureaucrats and sociologists much like himself. The service of humanity is the great end of all morality, and will be primarily fostered through the mother's training of the child in reverence and respect. If Comteanism proved something of a minor current in Irish intellectual life, the fact is perhaps not wholly to be regretted.

5

Young Irelanders and Others

Some of the major scholarly achievements of nineteenth-century Ireland, understandably enough, came in the field of Celtic studies. It was on this terrain above all that the Gaelic-Irish felt able to compete with an Anglo-Irish clerisy who monopolized much of the nation's intellectual life. Celtic antiquity, after all, was their own cultural heritage; their ability to read Irish was a signal advantage here; and such studies were hospitable to the amateur or autodidact as the sciences were not. John O'Donovan, known as the 'Fifth Master' for his monumental labour in editing and translating the *Annals of the Four Masters*, attended a hedge school as a child and then a classical school in Dublin, as good an education as a Catholic of limited means could obtain at the time. He also edited the Brehon laws with Eugene O'Curry, an immense and exacting assignment, wrote an important grammar of the Irish language and catalogued Trinity's collection of Celtic manuscripts. The college awarded him an honorary doctorate for his pains, though he would no doubt have preferred a decent income. He was in dire financial straits all his life, despondently thought of emigrating and was refused a government pension; a chair of Celtic Languages finally brought him a sorely needed annual salary of £100.[1] If the state had seen fit to support his prodigious labours, there is no telling to what greater heights he may have climbed.

O'Donovan, Ireland's greatest historical topographer, left behind him a sizeable pile of correspondence with the Ordnance Survey office in the course of tramping around Irish counties ascertaining the proper form of Irish place-names. Witty, affable and ironic, the letters read rather like a picaresque novel, as O'Donovan meets up with a motley crew of erudite parsons, cantankerous petty gentry and crazed clerics[2] in his hunt for philological accuracy. He breaks occasionally into dramatic dialogue, translates snatches of Irish verse into jocular doggerel and declares himself as much at home in an Ulster hamlet as in Dublin. Scorned by a few of his higher-class interlocutors as a Paddy, he says of himself that 'Milesian, Norman, and Cromwellian blood run [sic] through my veins. . . . I hope such a mixture is capable of forming a rational human being'.[3] Unflinchingly hostile to pedantry, he interweaves pen portraits worthy of a novelist into his antiquarian reflections. Nothing eludes his attention, as he follows up rumours that snakes have been spotted near Downpatrick while trying to economize on expenditure for the sake of his Dublin masters.

George Petrie, doyen of nineteenth-century Celtic studies, was often in hardly better financial shape than O'Donovan. But he was the acknowledged leader of the rather less socially glamorous Gaelic-Irish scholars, and in Vivian Mercier's view 'more important in the long run than Thomas Davis, Douglas Hyde, or perhaps even Yeats'.[4] No part of nineteenth-century cultural life in Ireland was untouched by his formidable influence. Indeed, it is hard to think of another intellectual of his period who rivalled his achievement, if not his scholarly scope. There is a case that Petrie was the single most important nineteenth-century Irish intellectual; he was certainly its most erudite palaeographer. Matthew Arnold praises him as one of a 'race of giants' in his *Study of Celtic Literature*. As painter, archaeologist, antiquarian, topographer, musicologist and indefatigable cultural activist,[5] Petrie was the tutelary spirit of the topographical section of the Ordnance Survey. He was awarded gold medals by the Royal Irish Academy for his pioneering *Essay on the Round Towers of Ireland* (1833) and *On the History and Antiquities of Tara Hill* (1839), and greatly augmented the resources of the Royal Irish Academy museum with such priceless masterpieces as the cross of Cong and a holograph copy of the *Annals of the Four Masters*. Some considered that he might well have been a great scientist had he turned his hand to that trade too.

Petrie's collections of Irish music played a major role in the Irish Revival, and his *The Ancient Music of Ireland* (1855) has been hailed as an intellectual landmark. Its composition involved a public, collaborative project typical of a certain kind of classical intellectual. The public were invited to send copies of still unwritten songs to a central Dublin depot, which Petrie then processed.[6] In this way, culture was passed upward from the people into the preservative hands of the intellectuals. An example of the process is a Kerry fiddler named Roche, who played a planxty composed by Carolan, which was copied down in a manuscript book of Irish airs by the amateur musicologist John Shannon of Listowel, to be discovered there by John Kelly of the Ordnance Survey, who passed it on to Petrie for its first publication. Thomas Moore used many of Petrie's airs, and Daniel O'Connell was known to have sung a few of them. It was not a project without its political implications. William Stokes remarks of Petrie that he was 'largely helpful towards achieving the great problem of our day – the reconciliation of the cultivated intelligence and loyalty, with the popular aspirations and the sympathies of the country'.[7] What was proving hard to achieve in political reality could always be pulled off by sharing a song. His work marks the point where the easy-going amateurism of the genteel antiquarian is yielding ground to a rigorous professionalism: as one commentator remarks, he 'cleared away the last vestiges of Vallancey's Celtomania and laid down a programme for Irish studies which errs openly on the side of austerity and realism'.[8] He was, in brief, the first major Irish archaeological revisionist, with a cold-eyed sobriety of judgement which some have related to his semi-outsider status as an Irish Scot.

Like many of his colleagues, Petrie was for the most part a state intellectual, employed by the British government on the Ordnance Survey and a member of bodies like the Royal Irish Academy, the Royal Hibernian Academy (where he regularly exhibited his sketches and watercolours) and the Irish Archaeological Society. The Ordnance Survey (1833–46) represents the rare spectacle of a batch of traditional Irish intellectuals – poets, clerics, academics, artists – being roped into a colossally ambitious colonialist project, enjoying an intimate collaboration with each other under the auspices of the state. Since some of this scholarship was to inspire later nationalist writers, it could be claimed that the Irish Revival was funded in part by the British state. It was the British government, for example, which undertook the publication of the Brehon laws. The encounter between state and traditional intelligentsia in the Ordnance Survey undertaking was not to prove entirely felicitous: one reason why the survey was closed down was the crushing weight of detail which these quasi-obsessive scholars supplied, a punctiliousness which lent the project 'Casaubonish proportions'.[9]

Within the *cameraderie* of this select band of scholars, however, a certain class-structure in miniature can be observed. 'In Petrie's study', writes Samuel Ferguson, 'I formed the acquaintance of O'Donovan, Curry [then without the O], and Mangan, and in the parlour of the Editor of the "University", of Stanford, Walker, Butt, the O'Sullivans, and later on of Wilde'.[10] But it is unlikely that Ferguson would have run into Mangan or O'Donovan at one of Butt's or Wilde's dinner parties, and Terence de Vere White doubts that Gaelic-Irish scholars like O'Donovan or O'Curry would have been invited to take part in R. P. Graves's Shakespearean *soirées*.[11] These Catholic scholars worked largely as subalterns to the gentry: O'Donovan, for example, taught Petrie Irish, and is described by him on their first meeting as 'in peasant garb'.[12] Samuel Ferguson waxes lyrical over the enterprise as a prototype of political conciliation: 'Is it not a delightful spectacle, now perhaps for the first time exhibited in Ireland, to see Irishmen of all parties and creeds, the most illustrious in rank and the most eminent in talents, combining zealously for an object of good to their common country?'[13] Cultural collaboration is a foretaste of social utopia, 'an auspicious omen of future happiness and peace'. In fact both projects, Ordnance Survey and class harmony, were to be aborted. Ferguson paints his impressions of Petrie and his acolytes crowded in the back parlour of the Ordnance Survey office: 'There was our venerable chief, with his ever-ready smile and gracious word; there poor Clarence Mangan, with his queer puns and jokes, and odd little cloak and wonderful hat'.[14] It is a clubbable gathering, but also a hierarchical one, as the word 'chief' would suggest. Petrie, in William Stokes's revealingly patronizing phrase, was the 'beloved master and teacher . . . [of] these genuine Irishmen, racy of the soil'.[15]

No sharper contrast with the painstaking factualism of Petrie's scholarly circle could be imagined than the writings of their hanger-on James Clarence Mangan, who as Alfred Graves points out in his *Literary and Musical Studies* would improve on his originals while translating because translation was what he lived by. It is the difference between the scholar's fidelity to his or her texts and the artist's free-wheeling recycling of them for his own devious ends. The Gothic Mangan, with his flaxen-coloured wig, waxen, Andy Warhol-like complexion, outsize green spectacles, false teeth, exotic hat and cloak, bottle of tar water, drugs, whiskey and two bulky umbrellas (one for each arm), was as flamboyantly inauthentic as some of his 'translations', a kind of proto-postmodern parody of the *poète maudit*. Like his mongrelized poetry, this bogus persona could also be seen as a wry comment on the precarious, 'intertextual' nature of colonial identity.[16] It was as though he could turn his own lack of selfhood to good use by recapitulating in his doomed career the bleakness of his entire epoch, all the way from dire poverty to death from fever. Precisely because he was so aberrant, he could become representative of a more general state of abjection.

Mangan's literary career was also a parodic commentary on a scholarly reverence for fact, which had not, after all, proved of unequivocal value to the Irish. In a society where the scrupulous collecting of social data had played its part in political control as well as in social enlightenment, the scholar's passion for fact could not be seen as entirely ideologically innocent. In any case, the facts in question were often enough rebarbative, distilling a human wretchedness belied by the impassive spirit in which they were studied. Just as the political revolutionary wants to change the facts, so Mangan felt free to reinvent them. While scholars bend their energies to what is the case, radicals turn them to what might be. This suspicion of the subjunctive mood is perhaps one reason for the politically conservative cast of so much academic scholarship. In John Mitchel's astute word, Mangan 'upset' the original materials into his own versions of them, practising a hermeneutical licence which was, ironically, fairly traditional in the history of Irish letters.[17] Some of his translations, his editor observes, pour wine from a leaden vessel into a golden goblet of strange and delicate fashioning.[18]

If Mangan was an author he was also an anti-author, who published only one book and stole much of the rest of his material. Mitchel comments that he 'took an elfish pleasure in belittling and parodying his great efforts'.[19] Some of his German translations are faithful, others fanciful, and a few of the original authors nonexistent. His verse theatricalizes the inner life with a crude power and an absence of half-lights, its despair too melodramatic and its hope too triumphalist. He swings with equal abruptness from the histrionic to the trivial, lurching from the ludic to the lugubrious with little middle ground. If one of his registers is the overpitched rhetoric of nationalism, the other is a vein of extravagant aimlessness to which, seen as a social condition, nationalism was one political response. It is hard for him to be serious and witty together, so that the seriousness lapses too often into portentousness and the wit degenerates into facetious trifling.[20] His humour is really a kind of frenetic desperation, in which it is not hard to detect a certain colonial futility and self-involvement. His very early verse casts knowing side-glances at itself in a jocular, Byronic kind of way, while his more laboured efforts have a less playful, more paralytic sort of self-consciousness about them. If his writing is not to shatter into squibs, doggerel, baroque flourishes or self-consuming wordplay, it needs the discipline of a tight metrical form, or of a target text on which to model itself. Mangan and Petrie may well have occupied the same office, but their sensibilities, like their politics, were worlds apart.

········

It has become customary in some modern Irish scholarship to contrast the judicious high seriousness of the *Dublin University Magazine* with the adolescent idealism of the *Nation*. Thomas Davis's nostalgic Romanticism, John Mitchel's savage Anglophobia and zeal for slavery, William Smith O'Brien's genteel blundering, Charles Gavan Duffy's portentous self-importance, Thomas Francis Meagher's embarrassingly purple oratory: these are hardly to be ranked with the august intellectual substance of the *DUM*. In fact, as we have seen, the *DUM* was by no means innocent of bigotry and partisanship, not least in its early years, while Young Ireland was a considerably more moderate, liberal-minded project than is sometimes suggested. A certain revisionist view of the movement thus stands in need of a little revision.

Young Ireland was not unreserved in its ardour for cultural nationalism. John Mitchel and Gavan Duffy, both Ulstermen, were mildly contemptuous of the creed. Thomas Davis was a devotee of the Irish language, in contrast with O'Connell's more pragmatic attitude to it: for him, English was an 'unnatural' as well as corrupting tongue for Celts to speak, and he implies in a quaint piece of nationalist physiology that Irish vocal organs are inadequately adapted to it. But he also regarded English as the first language of the island, at least for commercial purposes, while O'Connell occasionally used Irish himself and once spoke of it to his disciples as 'your proper language'. Nor were the Young Irelanders always parochial in their political scope. Davis wrote perceptively on India, in what was to become a long history of nationalist alliance between the two nations, and was also greatly preoccupied with Afghanistan. Fintan Lalor universalized the conflict in Ireland to one against colonialism in general, and speaks the language of the First International in his declaration that 'Mankind will yet be masters of the earth'.[21] The group could be embarrassingly starry-eyed or catastrophist about the nation's history, but Gavan Duffy can write caustically that 'in Ireland hitherto, history has repeated itself with the fidelity of a stock piece at the theatre, where nothing is changed from generation to generation but the actors'.[22]

The *Nation* rebuked potential contributors for glorifying violence, as well as for an inflated estimate of Irish capacities; a lengthy period of national education, it believed, was essential for genuine political freedom. Thomas Davis writes of the people's need to learn

133

literature, the arts and the disciplines of self-government in order to groom themselves for political independence, though he is shrewd enough to see that independence is itself 'the greatest teacher' in this respect. He refuses, in short, the classic colonialist view that the people are never quite ready to assume control of their own affairs, which neglects to mention colonialism itself as one major cause of this immaturity. Repelled by O'Connell's guileful softsoaping of the nation, the Young Irelanders neither pandered to the masses nor superciliously despised them.[23] A recurrent theme of Thomas Meagher's work is the need for the nation to find a faith in its own faculties which a history of colonialism had damaged. In this sense at least, the group were by no means Romantic idealists. Republicanism was not seriously advocated by any of their number, including John Mitchel, until 1848. As for revolutionary violence, even Mitchel's notorious newspaper piece recommending the pulling up of railway tracks for military purposes concerned purely defensive action. He warned the Irish people to avoid being the first to spill blood, declared in his newspaper the *United Irishman* that they would not do so and issued a prospectus which defended their right to bear arms but did not advocate warfare. He did, however, consider provoking the British government into using violence against the nationalist movement, thereby justifying military action on its own part.

For the most part, however, Young Ireland's stress on the legitimacy of defensive violence differed little from O'Connell's own pacifism. A well-bred gentleman like Davis was unlikely to greet the idea of mass insurgency with much relish. Meagher's celebrated chivalric speech on the place of the sword in nationalist combat was meant as a plea not to dismiss this option out of hand, not as a strategy to be zealously embraced. The speech makes it clear that armed force has not the slightest chance of success in 1840s Ireland: 'an incitement to arms would be senseless, and therefore wicked'.[24] Having first advocated military action to rescue Mitchel after his arrest, Meagher thought better of the proposal and withdrew it. Refusing to condemn violence out of hand was more a political ploy against the O'Connellites than a reflection of Young Ireland's sanguinary spirit. Ribbonism, for example, was anathema to the organization. Meagher has been mocked for the idle academicism of his encomium on the sword, but this too is questionable: he was later to prove a gallant officer in the Irish Brigade in the American Civil War, where he witnessed his men slaughtered around him in some of the bloodiest battles of the century.[25] Mitchel ended up embracing military action more as a desperate *acte gratuit* than a political programme. 'It is better to reduce the island to a cinder', he writes luridly to Lalor, 'than let it rot into an obscure quagmire, peopled with reptiles'.[26] Mitchel's cult of violence is ultimately an existential affair, a reckless attempt to goad a contemptibly craven nation into regaining its self-esteem. If this Sorelian doctrine is reprehensible in him, it is equally to be admonished in the later Yeats. Lalor adhered to the option of armed force as long as the British did too: 'Let England pledge not to argue the question by the prison, the convict-ship or the halter, and I will readily pledge not to argue it in any form of physical logic. But dogs tied and stones loose is no bargain'.[27]

As far as religion went, the Young Irelanders were on the whole impressively tolerant and pluralist. They supported denomination-ally mixed education, including the so-called godless colleges of Queen's university; indeed O'Connell himself was originally sym-pathetic to religious co-education. In general, they were hostile to any form of Catholic chauvinism or supremacism. They were also portrayed as soft on Unionism. Nor were they, politically speaking, especially radical. If O'Connell decried Chartism for both its vio-lence and social agenda, the *Nation* fulminated against some of the Charter's clauses as 'an abomination'. Though no socialist, Davis at one point proposed an alliance with the Chartists, but both Meagher and Mitchel repudiated Chartism as such. The Confederation, how-ever, as successor to the 'classical' period of Young Ireland, did indeed become involved with the Chartists, and by mid-1848 in England the two currents were well-nigh indistinguishable. The *Nation* occasionally ridiculed O'Connell's philosophical-radical lean-ings, even if O'Connell himself was by no means an out-and-out free trader. Meagher wished to bring the Irish peers and conserva-tives along with the Young Ireland project, paid homage to the crown and defended the necessity of social ranks and privileges. He was no republican, he insisted, and could not imagine a state without an aristocracy.[28] Instead, he desired a national movement which united all classes. He forswore all intention to harm property, a pledge that William Smith O'Brien duly acted upon in the 1848 insurrection when he forbade his troops to trespass on private land. The group continued to rally the landed gentry to political leadership of the nation even when those appeals were blatantly utopian. Thomas Davis called on the aristocracy to 'save the people', and even Mitchel shared this illusion as late as 1847. Mitchel also declared that he would not object to an Irish monarchy, and was neither a democrat nor a republican.

Like a good many other Irish radicals, then, the Young Irelanders were by and large a fairly conservative band. Compromise and confusion would seem more their hallmark than bigotry and fanaticism. They were harried, partly by the state's hounding of their members, into a disastrously premature uprising in a prostrate, famine-stricken society, an adventurist revolt which few of them thought likely to bear much fruit. Duffy wrote wryly to O'Brien that they would probably meet on a Jacobin scaffold as enemies of some new Marat or Robespierre, a prophecy which was later to be grimly realized in the case of the Republican opponents of the Irish Free State. Smith O'Brien's kid-gloved approach to revolution, his impeccably courteous attempt to overturn the state, was more a matter of *noblesse oblige* than Jacobin frenzy. Even James Fintan Lalor, their most socially radical member, was by no means a prototype of James Connolly. Like many an Irish nationalist, Lalor displayed a lofty contempt for politics and staked all on the land question. Politics was just 'paper and parchment', whereas his own rather less modest goal was to 'repeal the Conquest'. Indeed, he even wrote at one point to Robert Peel to announce his opposition to Repeal and to offer the Prime Minister his services. Shrewdly enough, he anticipated Parnell in coupling the land issue to the national question since he believed that Repeal – a largely urban doctrine in his view – would not in itself rouse the agricultural tenantry to decisive political action. Arthur Griffith did not consider him much of a nationalist. Politics finally overtook Lalor in the guise of an abortive *putsch* in Tipperary in 1849, in which he lay out all night to no observable military effect.

136

Lalor's position on the landlords, like that of Young Ireland in general, is notably inconsistent. An early champion of a cross-class national alliance, he later writes of the need to abolish the landowning class as such; but his vision of an Ireland in which all landed property is invested in the state, and then leased out to those who declare their allegiance to the nation, would seem at times to include the landlords too. In a letter to the *Nation*, he informs the landowners that they have the power to frame a new constitution, but in the same document speaks in Lockean terms of this power as residing in the people themselves. (As a devotee of Blackstone, Lalor was one of the few Irish nationalists to speak the discourse of natural rights rather than the Burkean language of custom and tradition: 'no generation of living men can bind a generation that is yet unborn, or can sell or squander the rights of man'.[29]) It is now up to the landed gentry to frame a 'new mode of living and labour', since with the Famine the present social order stands dissolved. But with typical Young Ireland ambivalence, he ends his letter on a note of class reconciliation: the landlords' rights and interests will be fully safeguarded under a new popular constitution. In a letter to Mitchel, however, he declares his life-long belief that the landowners are aliens and enemies, and chooses to appear duplicitous rather than inconsistent in maintaining that he held this view even when he appealed to them for leadership. Despite this dim view of the Irish patriciate, he would still, he declares, grant land titles to those of them who swore fealty to the nation. In his *Felon Letters*, his position has shifted once more: the landlords are now a 'garrison' who should be summarily expelled. 'They or we must quit this island'.[30]

Lalor was a self-conscious revolutionary who criticized John Mitchel's brand of uprising as anarchic. He believed Repeal to be an absurd impracticality, since Britain and Ireland could not be both linked and independent; the Act of Union, he maintained, would never be repealed by law. But for the most part he is not even interested enough in the Repeal question to wish to refute the proposal, and in the *Felon Letters* declares that he is not against it as such. It is just that it must be combined with the land issue if it is not to remain an elitist affair, appealing to the skilled but not to the common labourer. The Confederation, Lalor considered with some justification, wished to preserve aristocracy and achieve a national but not democratic revolution. His judgement certainly turned out to be true of the Land League. Thomas Davis looked askance on social (though not political) equality, while Duffy held the elitist urban opinion that the agricultural tenantry could never politically organize themselves. If Lalor thought industrialization both inevitable and desirable, his view of it as inherently beneficial was scarcely shared by the more narodnik of the Young Irelanders.

Much of John Mitchel's supposed radicalism was in fact a thinly disguised form of conservatism. As Christopher Morash puts it, he 'refused Enlightenment'.[31] If he came to believe in the need for social revolution, he also regarded it as a necessary evil. He was resolutely opposed to underground conspiracies – their secrets, he thought, were what gave them away – and dissented from Fenianism even though he once did a spot of work on its behalf in Paris. He turned down the post of chief executive officer of the American Fenian Brotherhood, and differed from the Fenians not least in his belief that Northern Protestants must be rallied to the nationalist cause. His Anglophobia, as with a good deal of Irish nationalism, was in some ways less an abhorrence of the English than a hatred of modernity as such, a Carlylean contempt for commerce, manufacture and the 'cant' of progress and benevolence which sits as easily on the right as on the left. It led Mitchel himself in both directions at once: towards an autocratic anti-liberalism, as well as to a belief that the poor must not be abandoned to the mercy of the rich. His *Jail Journal* distinguishes between the English people and what he calls the 'Thing', meaning the political system; he is, he declares, a friend rather than a foe of England, and believes its people have themselves suffered because of the empire.

Mitchel's hostility to industrial capitalism also helps to explain (if not excuse) his enthusiasm for the slavery of the southern American states, which he obtusely misinterprets as a form of *gemeinschaftlich* bonding between masters and servants in contrast to the heartless cash-nexus of industrial capitalism. The southern states thus become a kind of Ireland confronting an exploitative industrial north which resembles England. Two of Mitchel's sons were slain in the American Civil War, one of them at Gettysburg, and he himself was actively involved as a propagandist and ambulance assistant on the defeated side. When he was arrested and imprisoned for some months after the civil war, he remarked that he was the only person to have been a prisoner of state first in Britain and then in the USA. As a man, he was said to be gentle, agreeable and compassionate.[32]

If the Young Irelanders were not among the most coherent of Irish political thinkers, they were certainly among the finest stylists. Here, for example, is Mitchel's description of the victims of famine:

> Children met you, toiling heavily on stone-heaps, but their burning eyes were senseless, and their faces cramped and weasened like stunted old men. Gangs worked, but without a murmur, or a whistle, or a laugh, ghostly, like voiceless shadows to the eye. Even womanhood had ceased to be womanly. The birds of the air carolled no more, and the crow and the raven dropped dead upon the wing. The very dogs, hairless, with the head down, and the vertebrae of the back protruding like a saw of bone, glared on you from the ditch-side with a wolfish avid eye, and then slunk away scowling and cowardly.[33]

If this has its set-piece features, surrendering to theatrical cliché in the odd phrase ('wolfish avid eye', 'scowling and cowardly'), the broken syntax of the second sentence and the image of 'voiceless shadows' suggests a spectral crumbling of reality, at once baldly factual and hauntingly uncanny. 'Voiceless shadows' is in one sense a tautology, since one does not expect shadows to have voices anyway; but it also superbly blends the dimming of two faculties together, as the body's sounds fade along with its substance. The calculated rhythmical symmetry of 'The birds of the air carolled no more, and the crow and the raven dropped dead on the wing', with its emblematic, quasi-scriptural overtones, is instantly counterpointed by a limping, dragging, broken-backed sentence which seems consciously to sacrifice literary equipoise to descriptive authenticity.

Thomas Meagher was aware of Young Ireland's eloquence, and satirizes the way it was mangled in police reports: 'An eloquent speech is enough, of itself, to disorganise the police force of Ireland. A metaphor brings on giddiness of the brain; an allusion to the shield of Achilles, or the trumpet of Alecto, induces the worst symptoms of suffocation; blank verse bogs them; an antithesis starts a

139

sinew; and as for an apostrophe! it is sure to give them sciatica, or the lock-jaw'.[34] It is a matter of speech versus the body, just as Young Ireland itself was caught in a contradiction between oratory and action. Part of Meagher's point here is to show that he and his colleagues are not just hollow rhetoricians – that they are ironically conscious of the farcical gap between their own grandiloquent verbal flights and the quotidian world, but are not thereby prepared to abandon that rhetoric as merely ludicrous. If society cannot measure up to their elaborate periods, that is a judgement on it rather than on them. Rather as Mitchel feels a draining of reality in the Famine, so Meagher has a similar hallucinatory sense during the 1848 uprising, as the Young Ireland insurgents enter the town of Carrick:

> A torrent of human beings rushing through lanes and narrow streets; surging and boiling against the white basements that hemmed it in; whirling in dizzy circles, and tossing up its dark waves, with sounds of wrath, vengeance, and defiance; clenched hands, darting high above the black and broken surface, and waving to and fro, with the wildest confusion, in the air; eyes red with rage and desperation, starting and flashing upwards through the billows of the flood; long tresses of hair – disordered, drenched, and tangled – streaming in the roaring wind of voices, and, as in a shipwreck, rising and falling with the foam.[35]

In a familiar trope of political turmoil, the world dissolves to a dishevelled dream at its most intense moment of reality, and Meagher's stumbling syntax reproduces this sense of fragmentation. There is a hint of the sublime here, as horror and excitement, fascination and repulsion, mingle in the radical middle-class observer of this popular riot. The scene can only be grasped as a whole through metaphorical displacement, as the streets become a seascape and human beings are naturalized to a boiling torrent or dismembered to bits of limbs and gestures. The senses are disrupted, as tresses of hair stream in a wind of voices, and the crowd presents itself at once as a collective body and a set of sensory fragments, mere flotsam and jetsam on the waves of its own activity. A sense of unified purpose and one of chaos are thus curiously fused. In one

140

sense the mutinous crowd is out of control, swept helplessly along by a depth which is invisible to the spectatorial eye; in another sense, this unfathomable abyss is nothing but its own actions, so that what buoys it up is itself. The whole scene is at once intensely present and aesthetically distanced, as the observer 'frames' it with a metaphor of storm and shipwreck which both heightens its effect and fends off its destructive force. The human torrent itself is similarly contained, though only just, by the narrow lanes within which it ferments.

Few groups of intellectuals have had such a spectacular impact on politics as Young Ireland. John Mitchel claims that 'this band of literary revolutionists' had 'the ear of the people almost as completely as O'Connell himself',[36] and not many pieces of newsprint have created such historical turmoil as the *Nation*. We may note, finally, how many of the Young Irelanders hailed from backgrounds rather different to those of Stokes and Wilde. Mitchel was born near Dungiven, County Derry, Duffy was from Monaghan, Lalor from the provincial, agrarian middle class, while Thomas Davis, as the son of an Englishman of Welsh extraction and a woman of both Gaelic and Cromwellian descent, was a walking symbol of ethnic diversity. Two other members of the band were exceptional for their patrician origins: Meagher, son of the lord mayor and Member of Parliament for Waterford, was educated at Clongowes and Stonyhurst, while William Smith O'Brien was Oxford-educated and upper-class English in cultural style. In one way or another, whether social, ethnic, regional or denominational, these men stood counter to the dominant *milieu* of Anglo-Irish Dublin. It is worth noting too that in the intellectual history of nineteenth-century Ireland, Mitchel, Duffy, Ferguson, Carleton, Kells Ingram, Sigerson, George Russell and Eoinn Mac Neill all stemmed from Ulster, while Petrie (the son of an Aberdonian numismatist) and Hamilton (more remotely) were of Scottish ancestry. But the curiously energetic presence of Ulster intellectuals in Dublin life would require another study.

141

Notes

Chapter 1 Colonial Intellectuals

1 It was on an Irish author, the socialist and feminist William Thompson, that Karl Marx drew in the first volume of *Capital* to discuss the division of manual and mental labour. Marx quotes a reference by Thompson to the separation of the man of intellect from the productive labourer, by which knowledge becomes 'an instrument, capable of being detached from labour and opposed to it'.

2 Isaac Butt, *Intellectual Progress* (Limerick, 1872), p. 22.

3 W. E. H. Lecky, *Historical and Political Essays* (London, 1908), p. 105.

4 Both features can be found in some of the major intellectuals of our time: Habermas, Chomsky, Williams, Kristeva, Jameson, Foucault, Bourdieu, Anderson, Said, Derrida.

5 A rare and useful essay on Dowden is to be found in Terence Brown, *Ireland's Literature* (Dublin, 1988).

6 T. W. Heyck, *The Transformation of Intellectual Life in Victorian England* (London, 1982), p. 24.

7 See Raymond Williams, *Keywords* (London, 1976), pp. 140–2.

8 The intellectual/intelligentsia distinction is a vexed one. Liam O'Dowd reserves the term 'intelligentsia' for a technical, specialist class, while 'intellectuals' are those members of the intelligentsia 'who concern themselves with social questions beyond the remit of their own specialised area of knowledge' ('Intellectuals and Political Culture: A Unionist–Nationalist Comparison', in Eamonn Hughes (ed.), *Culture and Politics in Northern Ireland 1960–1990* (Milton Keynes, 1991)). This

would make intellectuals 'critical' and the intelligentsia the handmaidens of a particular social order, as against the original Russian sense of 'intelligentsia'. Tom Bottomore distinguishes between the educated professionals of an intelligentsia and those 'intellectuals' more narrowly concerned with the creation and transmission of ideas (*Elites and Society*, London, 1964, p. 64). Anthony D. Smith sees the intelligentsia as a vocational or professional group who 'live off the cultural capital generated by intellectuals' – the executive wing of the creators of ideas, so to speak (*The Ethnic Revival*, Cambridge, 1981, p. 108f).

9   See John Hutchinson, *The Dynamics of Cultural Nationalism* (London, 1987), p. 261, and R. B. McDowell, *The Irish Administration 1801–1914* (London, 1964), which traces the immense reform, expansion and professionalization of the Irish civil service earlier in the century. McDowell notes that 'As early as 1833 the Treasury directed departments to take steps to ensure that persons appointed to vacancies in them should be qualified to perform their duties' (p. 23), a revoutionary innovation indeed.

10   Gramsci distinguishes in his writings between those 'traditional' intellectuals like clerics, academics and philosophers who claim a certain autonomous, transhistorical status, and those 'organic' intellectuals who, as representatives of a (usually emergent) social class, define their tasks in conjunctural, activist, organizational ways. See Quintin Hoare and Geoffrey Nowell Smith (eds), *Selections from the Prison Notebooks of Antonio Gramsci* (London, 1971), pp. 5–23.

11   For the Ordnance Survey, see John Andrews, *A Paper Landscape* (Oxford, 1975), and Joep Leersen, *Remembrance and Imagination* (Cork, 1996), pp. 101–6. For a more critical view of the project, see Mary Hamer, 'Putting Ireland on the Map', *Textual Practice*, vol. 3, no. 2 (1989).

12   For a modern Irish defence of this phenomenon, penned by a dissident, Arnoldian Anglo-Irish intellectual in the days of militant Gaelic nationalism, see John Eglinton, *Two Essays on the Remnant* (Dublin, 1894). This elegant, melancholic monograph argues that the intellectual elite, now wholly displaced from civil society, must simply go out into the wilderness, 'unfit and unemployed'. This elite was once the leaven of society, fulfilling *à la* Goethe a vital social function; but in the modern era intellectuals must discover their *raison d'être* in themselves.

13   The nineteenth-century Irish scholar Dionysius Lardner is said to have proved by purely mathematical means the impossibility of steamship travel between Ireland and the United States just at the point when it was getting under way. See W. J. Fitzpatrick, *Life of Charles Lever*

(London, 1879), vol. 1, p. 50.

14 See Gramsci, *Prison Notebooks*, pp. 5–8.

15 For Burke and sentiment, see Terry Eagleton, *Crazy John and the Bishop* (Cork, 1998), chapter 3, pp. 133–9. This is not, of course, to suggest that Burke's traditionalism was entirely of Irish origin, rather that his rhetorical appeals to English traditionalism were intensified by it.

16 For one of the most intricate understandings of these paradoxes, see Seamus Deane, 'Edmund Burke and Liberalism', in Richard Kearney (ed.), *The Irish Mind* (Dublin, 1985).

17 The standard study of the man of letters is John Gross, *The Rise and Fall of the Man of Letters* (London, 1969). See also A. J. Beljame, *Men of Letters and the English Public in the Eighteenth Century* (London, 1931), Louis Dudek, *Literature and the Press* (Toronto, 1960) and, for an useful account of the English Victorian scene, Christopher Kent, 'Higher Journalism and the Mid-Victorian Clersity', *Victorian Studies*, no. 13 (1969).

18 For Carlyle and Young Ireland, see Christopher Morash, 'Imagining the Famine: Literary Representations of the Great Irish Famine' (PhD thesis, Trinity College, Dublin, 1990).

19 See Heyck, p. 41.

20 Jacqueline Hill calculates the Irish intelligentsia of the 1840s at around a mere 1 per cent of the working population, in a period when less than half of the Irish could read and write. See her 'The Intelligentsia and Irish Nationalism in the 1840s', *Studia Hibernica*, no. 20 (1980). Isaac Butt considered the backwardness of the division of material labour in Ireland to be a prime cause of the country's lack of civility: if each tenant farmer was more or less self-sufficient, the mutual dependence to which we owe 'all the progress of the most refined civilisation' could not get under way. See Isaac Butt, *A Voice for Ireland: the Famine in the Land* (Dublin, 1847), p. 32.

21 Liam O'Dowd, 'Intellectuals in 20th Century Ireland: the Case of George Russell (AE)', *The Crane Bag*, vol. 9, no. 1, Dublin, 1985, p. 9.

22 The comment occurs in Mc Cormack's Appendix to Donal McCartney's *W. E. H. Lecky: Historian and Politician 1838–1903* (Dublin, 1994), p. 201.

23 For a survey of the English man of letters, see Terry Eagleton, *The Function of Criticism* (London, 1984).

24 O'Dowd, p. 8.

25 See John Pentland Mahaffy, *Kant's Critical Philosophy* (London, 1874), a compact, lucid and not unintelligent exposition of some of Kant's leading ideas.

26 Alfred Perceval Graves, *Irish Literary and Musical Studies* (London, 1913), p. 37.

27 Owen Dudley Edwards in J. McCormack (ed.), *Wilde the Irishman*

NOTES TO PAGES 14–17

28 See J. B. Bury, *Life of Saint Patrick and His Place in History* (London, 1905).

29 See Terence de Vere White, *The Road to Excess* (Dublin, 1946).

30 See John Kells Ingram, 'On the "Weak Endings" of Shakespeare', *Transactions of the New Shakespeare Society*, series 1, no. 2, London, 1874. With typical Positivist zeal, Ingram appends to his piece a table of the number of weak line-endings in all of the plays, along with a calculation of the number of verse lines of each play.

31 The lecture is collected in *Afternoon Lectures on English Literature at the Museum of Industry in Dublin* (Dublin, 1863).

32 Vivian Mercier, *Modern Irish Literature* (Oxford, 1994), p. 1.

33 Joseph Raftery, 'George Petrie, 1789–1866: a Reassessment', *Proceedings of the Royal Irish Academy*, vol. 72, section C, no. 6 (Dublin, 1972).

34 John Tyndall, *Address Delivered before the British Association at Belfast* (London, 1874), p. 64. The address, which was thought to endorse Darwinism and atheistic materialism, and took a smack at Christian scholasticism, proved highly controversial.

35 W. K. Sullivan, 'On the Influence of Physical Causes on Languages, Mythology Etc.', *Atlantis*, vol. 2, London, 1859.

36 Liam O'Dowd, 'Intellectuals and Political Culture', pp. 155–6.

37 An improbable enthusiast of the Catholic University was the left-wing Young Irelander John Mitchel. See his *History of Ireland* (Dublin, 1869), vol. 2, pp. 475–6.

38 John Henry Newman, *The Idea of a University* (London, 1881), pp. xv–xvi. The poet Shelley shares Newman's perception of the Irish as hotblooded and immoderate, in his Dublin address of 1812. Gramsci actually copied into his prison notebooks some remarks from Newman's *The Idea of a University* about the need for clear, systematic and disciplined thought, thus demonstrating the natural alliance between the Marxist and the Catholic. See Derek Boothman (ed.), *Antonio Gramsci: Further Selections from the Prison Notebooks* (London, 1995), p. 151. Gramsci also notes the need for a study of the clergy as an intellectual caste (pp. 8–12).

39 Peadar O'Donnell described the Catholic hierarchy as a danger to Catholicism in Ireland. See Michael McInerney, *Paedar O'Donnell* (Dublin, 1974), p. 84.

40 Ibid., p. xxii.

41 Ibid., p. 101.

42 See John Henry Newman, *My Campaign in Ireland* (Aberdeen, 1896). Newman did, however, instantly establish chemistry, engineering, medicine and modern languages at the Catholic University, hardly the typical behaviour of a traditionalist.

43 Karl Mannheim, *Ideology and Utopia* (London, 1936), p. 136.
44 O'Dowd, p. 8.
45 Anthony D. Smith, *National Identity* (London, 1991), pp. 64 and 84.
46 See David Cairns and Shaun Richards, *Writing Ireland* (Manchester, 1988), pp. 42–57.
47 Tom Nairn, *The Break-up of Britain* (London, 1977), p. 102.
48 Ibid., p. 340.
49 *Prison Notebooks*, p. 453.
50 See George Petrie, *The Ecclesiastical Architecture of Ireland* (Dublin, 1845).
51 Harry White, *The Keeper's Recital* (Cork, 1998), p. 64.
52 Anthony D. Smith, *The Ethnic Origins of Nations* (Oxford, 1986), p. 161.
53 See Jean Archer, 'Scientific Loners: the *Journal of the Geological Society of Dublin* and Its Successors', in B. Hayley and E. MacKay (eds), *300 Years of Irish Periodicals* (Dublin, 1987), pp. 50–1. See also Gramsci, *Prison Notebooks*, pp. 6, 60, 334. There are also scattered comments on intellectuals in the two volumes of Gramsci's *Letters from Prison*, ed. Frank Rosengarten and Raymond Rosenthal (New York, 1994).
54 *Nations and Nationalism*, p. 31.
55 Thomas Davis, *Address Read before the Historical Society* (Dublin, 1840), p. 44.
56 See Thomas Duddy, in Tadhg Foley and Sean Rider (eds), *Ideology and Ireland in the Nineteenth Century Ireland* (Dublin, 1998), p. 145.
57 The phrase is Francis Mulhern's, in his *The Present Lasts a Long Time* (Cork, 1998), p. 91. Mannheim's idea of the disinterested intellectual is advanced in his *Ideology and Utopia* (London, 1929). For Sartre's reflections on the intelligentsia, see his *What Is Literature?* (London, 1950) and 'A Plea for Intellectuals', in *Between Existentialism and Marxism* (London, 1974).
58 Davis writes that a society for the arts will embrace men of every rank, class and creed, 'thus forming another of those sanctuaries, now multiplying in Ireland, where one is safe from the polemic and the partisan' ('National Art', in T. W. Rolleston (ed.), *Thomas Davis: Selections from his Prose and Poetry* (London, 1914), p. 167. Davis fails to mention that much of the polemic and partisanship stemmed from himself. One might note that a later nationalist, Patrick Pearse, shared something of this ecumenical vision. He spoke with enthusiasm of nations like Hungary, Belgium and Austria, where different languages, creeds and religions flourished side by side. Pearse was by no means the fanatical ethnic purist he has been sometimes painted as.
59 Isaac Butt, 'Past and Present State of Literature in Ireland', reprinted in Seamus Deane (ed.), *The Field Day Anthology of Irish Writing* (Derry, 1991), vol. 1, pp. 1200–12.
60 See Jürgen Habermas, *Strukturwandel der Öffentlichkeit* (Neuwied, 1962).

61 For the idea of a counter-public sphere, see Oskar Negt and Alexander Kluge, *Öffentlichkeit und Erfahrung: Zur Organisationsanalyse von burgerlicher und proletarischer Öffentlichkeit* (Frankfurt-am-Main, 1972).

62 W. J. Mc Cormack, in Seamus Deane (ed.), *The Field Day Anthology of Irish Writing* (Derry, 1988), vol. 1, p. 1176.

63 Michael Sadleir, '*Dublin University Magazine*: Its History, Components and Bibliography', *Bibliographical Society of Ireland*, vol. 5, no. 4, Dublin, 1938, pp. 54 and 67.

64 Thomas Davis, 'Ballad Poetry of Ireland', in *Literary and Historical Essays* , pp. 221–2.

65 See Terry Eagleton, 'Culture and Politics in Nineteenth-century Ireland', in *Heathcliff and the Great Hunger* (Oxford, 1995).

66 Quoted by Hutchinson, p. 79.

67 One should add, however, since the hapless Arnold has become such a predictable *bête noire* for today's cultural left, that his cultural interests were far more practical, and his view of academic English far more sceptical, than most of them seem to imagine.

68 Smith, *The Ethnic Origins of Nations*, p. 157.

69 Marianne Elliot, *Wolfe Tone: Prophet of Independence* (New Haven, CT, and London, 1989), p. 65.

70 Thomas Bartlett, 'The Burden of the Present: Wolfe Tone, Republican and Separatist', in David Dickson, Daire Keogh and Kevin Whelan (eds), *The United Irishmen: Republicanism, Radicalism and Rebellion* (Dublin, 1993).

71 See M. F. Cusack (ed.), *The Speeches and Public Letters of the Liberator* (Dublin, 1875), 2 vols. See also O'Connell's *Memoir on Ireland* (Dublin, 1843), which though dedicated to the queen reminds her semi-seditiously in its preface of English plunder and massacre in Ireland, and darkly warns that Ireland has a deep and vital interest in English weakness.

72 Patrick Pearse, *Political Writings and Speeches* (Dublin, 1922), p. 240.

73 Ibid., p. 241.

74 See Charles Gavan Duffy, *Thomas Davis: Memoirs of an Irish Patriot 1840–1846* (London, 1890), p. 120.

75 John Mitchel, *The Last Conquest of Ireland (Perhaps)* (Dublin, 1861, reprinted Galsgow, n.d.), p. 83.

76 See, for Thompson's writings, Dolores Dooley, *Equality in Community* (Cork, 1996), Richard K. P. Pankhurst, *William Thompson* (London, 1954) and Desmond Fennell, 'Irish Socialist Thought', in Richard Kearney (ed.), *The Irish Mind* (Dublin, 1985).

77 Ernest A. Boyd, *Appreciations and Depreciations* (Dublin and London, 1917), p. 115.

78 Quoted in Norman Atkinson, *Irish Education* (Dublin, 1969), p. 123.

79 W. E. H. Lecky, *History of European Morals from Augustus to Charlemagne* (London, 1869, reprinted New York, 1870), vol. 2, p. 206.

80 See *The Autobiography and Life of George Tyrrell* (London, 1912), vol. 1 by Tyrrell, vol. 2 by M. D. Petrie. For a graphic account of the intellectual oppressiveness of the Irish Catholic church, see W. P. Ryan, *The Pope's Green Island* (London, 1912).

81 Boyd, p. 115.

82 One of the most prominent Irish playwrights of the eighteenth century, Charles Macklin, was a Protestant convert from Catholicism. 'Macklin' was originally 'McLaughlin'. See Christopher J. Wheatley, '"Our own good, plain, old Irish English": Charles Macklin (Cathal McLaughlin) and Protestant Convert Accommodations', *Bullaun*, vol. 4, no. 1 (Autumn 1998).

83 Luke Gibbons has some perceptive comments on this shift, properly disowning the notion of some temperamental Irish incapacity for abstract thought, in Seamus Deane (ed.), *The Field Day Anthology of Irish Writing* (Derry, 1991), vol. 2, p. 950.

84 Duffy, p. 43.

85 Mercier, p. 44.

86 These schools, moreover, can be seen as conspiring to cut Catholics off from parts of their native cultural heritage, and thus to disable their cultural capacities in this way too. See David Fitzpatrick's essay 'The Futility of History: a Failed Experiment in Irish Education', in Ciaran Brady (ed.), *Ideology and the Historians* (Dublin, 1991).

87 For a useful account, see Norman Atkinson, *Irish Education* (Dublin, 1969).

88 See T. J. McElligott, *Education in Ireland* (Dublin, 1966), p. 13.

89 See Richard J. Finneran (ed.), *Letters of James Stephens* (New York, 1974), p. 151.

90 See Alan Warner, *William Allingham* (Lewisburg, PA, 1975), p. 46.

91 W. E. H. Lecky, *Political and Historical Essays* (London, 1908), p. 2.

92 William Steuart Trench's *The Realities of Irish Life* (London, 1869) also tends to reverse the trend, as its social and political analysis swerves constantly into fiction and imaginary dialogue.

93 L. Fogarty (ed.), *Fintan Lalor: Collected Writings* (Washington, DC, 1997).

94 See Vivian Mercier's discussion of Synge in his *Modern Irish Literature* (Oxford, 1994).

95 Though O'Grady himself drew upon Eugene O'Curry's *Lectures on the Manuscript Materials of Ancient Irish History* (1861), a work which – since it also influenced Ferguson, Yeats, Hyde, Synge, George Russsell and Lady Gregory – is nominated by Vivian Mercier as 'the prime source-text of the Literary Revival' (*Modern Irish Literature*, p. 16).

96 For a useful study of O'Grady, see Edward A. Hagan, *High Nonsensical*

Words: a Study of the Works of Standish O'Grady (New York, 1986). See also Philip L. Marcus, *Standish O'Grady* (Lewisburg, PA, 1970).

97 Though this also belonged to a laudable effort to lend politics a spiritual or philosophical depth beyond their sometimes unreflective immediacy, as T. S. Eliot's journal the *Criterion* would seek later to do in England. Besides, the Revival was to produce some impressive intellectual documents: see, for example, George Russell's 'Thoughts for a Convention' in his *Imaginations and Reveries* (Dublin and London, 1921), with its shrewd understanding of the politics of Protestant Ulster. A parallel perceptiveness about Ulster is rather surprisingly revealed in the Irish Irelander Arthur Clery's *The Idea of a Nation* (Dublin, 1907).

98 It might also be possible to see in Shaw's socialist corporatism a dim resonance of a pre-industrial Irish culture less marked by the ideology of individualism – though Bertolt Brecht once remarked that he had never laughed so much in his life as when he was told that Shaw was a socialist. Something of the same oblique approach to the emotions is present in Irish drama as a whole, which is typically stylizing and distancing rather than warm-bloodedly Romantic. It is a theatre of display rather than intimate exploration, with a stringent sense of form and a suspicion of raw feeling. Samuel Beckett's scrupulously choreographed drama carries this to a parodic extreme. See also Frank O'Connor's claim that 'Merely because the similarity of language always threatens to suck the [Irish] writer into the forms of the more highly evolved literature, he has to adopt every device to keep his distance from it' (*The Backward Look,* London, 1967, p. 146).

99 For this mode of argument, see Ernest Gellner, *Nations and Nationalism* (Oxford, 1983). Gellner even goes as far as to regard nationalism, implausibly, as a mode of resolving a conflict within the intelligentsia between its traditional and modernizing wings. For parallel arguments, see his *Thought and Change* (London, 1964).

100 See Benedict Anderson, *Imagined Communities* (London, 1983).

101 Elie Kedourie, *Nationalism* (London, 1960), p. 70.

102 Anthony D. Smith, *Theories of Nationalism* (London, 1971), p. 124.

103 Gramsci himself sometimes sees the organic intellectual as springing from the group or class he represents, and this is often the way the concept has been understood; but there seems to me no necessity for this interpretation, if the idea of function is to be fully emphasized.

104 Davitt was a typical self-taught working-class intellectual, as well as a stylish and perceptive writer. See in particular the splendid satire in *Leaves from a Prison Diary* (London, 1885), which inverts the political relations of Britain and Ireland, imagining a Britain ruled by an Irish viceroy in which it was treasonable to sing 'Rule, Britannia' or teach

English history in schools. See also T. W. Moody, *Davitt and the Irish Revolution* (Oxford, 1981).

105   *Prison Notebooks*, p. 6.

106   Ibid., p. 10.

107   Ibid., p. 3. Another reason for the instability of Gramsci's distinction is that if traditional intellectuals are only apparently independent of social interests, they may in fact be organic ones who conceal this status, from themselves perhaps as well as from others. And those who now appear as traditional to a rising social class were themselves perhaps organic in their time.

108   Quoted in Horace Wyndham, *Speranza: a Biography of Lady Wilde* (London, 1951), p. 160.

109   Ibid., p. 334.

110   Ibid., p. 60.

111   See Sean O'Faolain, *King of the Beggars* (London, 1938), p. 38.

112   Maguire wrote a rather eccentric, apocalyptic pamphlet warning of the dire effects of Home Rule. See *The Effects of Home Rule on the Higher Education* (Dublin, 1886), in which he claims that Britain would suffer economically from Irish Home Rule by having to step up military spending in the event of an enemy power using Ireland as a base for attack. For a taste of his philosophy, see *The Parmenides of Plato* (Dublin, 1882) and *The External Worlds of Sir William Hamilton and Dr Thomas Brown* (Dublin, 1868). See also Timothy P. Foley, 'Thomas Maguire and the Parnell Forgeries', *Journal of the Galway Archaeological and Historical Society*, no. 67 (1994), and Thomas Duddy, 'The Peculiar Opinions of an Irish Platonist: the Life and Thought of Thomas Maguire', in Foley and Ryder (eds), *Ideology and Ireland in the Nineteenth Century*.

113   See Lady Ferguson, *Sir Samuel Ferguson in the Ireland of His Day* (Edinburgh and London, 1896), vol. 1, p. 239.

Chapter 2 Portrait of a Clerisy

1   Noel Annan, *Leslie Stephen* (London, 1951), p. 1.

2   Quoted by Raymond Williams, 'The Bloomsbury Fraction', in *Problems in Materialism and Culture* (London, 1980), p. 149.

3   Ibid., p. 154.

4   Ibid., p. 155.

5   See Vivian Mercier, *Modern Irish Literature* (Oxford, 1994), Ch. 3.

6   Williams, p. 159.

7   Ibid., p. 160.

8   John Butler Yeats, *Early Memories* (Dublin, 1923), p. 88. As far as the affinity between Dublin and ancient Greece goes, Oscar Wilde wrote

of his mentor John Pentland Mahaffy's *Greek Life* that it 'attempts to treat the Hellenic world as Tipperary writ large'. For a life of Mahaffy, see W. B. Standford and R. B. McDowell, *Mahaffy: A Biography of an Anglo-Irishman* (London, 1971).

9   Though Yeats perhaps overestimates the prevalence of this virtue in Dublin too.

10   Ibid., p. 87.

11   Ibid., p. 92.

12   The phrase is Perry Anderson's, in his *The Origins of Postmodernity* (London, 1998), p. 85. For Anderson, this classical bourgeoisie is now almost extinct. The solid burghers of Thomas Mann, who survived long into post-Second World War Europe, have given way to 'an aquarium of floating, evanescent forms – the projectors and managers, auditors and janitors, administrators and speculators of contemporary capital: functions of a monetary universe that knows no social fixities or stable identities'.

13   Sir Robert Ball was a Cambridge astronomer, while his brother Valentine was director of the National Museum of Dublin. Their younger brother was a distinguished Dublin medic. Their father was an eminent naturalist who died in the museum of the Royal Irish Academy by rupturing a blood vessel while trying to sound one of the museum's antique bronze trumpets. Antiquarianism in Ireland could be a perilous business.

14   David Thornley's *Isaac Butt and Home Rule* (London, 1964, p. 17) quotes Thomas McNevin as describing the school of Butt and Ferguson as 'Orange Young Ireland'.

15   William Dillon, *Life of John Mitchel* (London, 1882), vol. 1, p. 64.

16   Lady Ferguson, *Sir Samuel Ferguson in the Ireland of His Day* (Edinburgh and London, 1896), vol. 1, p. 141.

17   W. J. Mc Cormack, *Sheridan Le Fanu and Victorian Ireland* (Oxford, 1980), p. 12.

18   Ibid., p. 145.

19   See William Gregory, *Autobiography* (London, 1894), pp. 64–74. Gregory was not, however, an unqualified conservative: in this work, he criticizes the British government for depending so heavily on private enterprise during the Famine, and though he opposed the Land League he supported tenant proprietorship.

20   Terence de Vere White, *The Anglo-Irish* (London, 1972), p. 181. For a later account of upper-middle-class life in Dublin, see Enid Starkie, *A Lady's Child* (London, 1941).

21   Ernie O'Malley, *On Another Man's Wound* (London, 1936), p. 24.

22   John B. Yeats, *Essays Irish and American* (Dublin and London, 1918), p. 34.

23 Lady Ferguson, vol. 1, p. 268.

24 Ibid., vol. 2, p. 232.

25 John P. Mahaffy, *The Principles of the Art of Conversation* (London, 1887), p. vii.

26 Ibid., p. 3.

27 Ibid., p. 84.

28 John Pentland Mahaffy, *Social Life in Greece* (London, 1874), p. 299.

29 Mahaffy, *Principles of the Art of Conversation*, p. 69. A case in point might be R. A. Anderson, who in forty-five years in Ireland as the henchman of Horace Plunkett never once called him by his first name. See his jolly anecdotal account of this period in his *With Sir Horace Plunkett in Ireland* (London, 1935).

30 Standford and McDowell, p. 191.

31 Quoted by Marianne Elliott, *Wolfe Tone: Prophet of Independence*, p. 145.

32 For a study of the poet, see Alan Warner, *William Allingham: An Introduction* (Dublin, 1971). See also Alfred Perceval Graves's perceptive essay on the poet in *Irish Literary and Musical Studies* (London, 1913), which notes that Ruskin praised him highly and Emerson quoted him at length. The poet Lionel Johnson observed that some of Allingham's poems resonate of Ireland without ever mentioning the place.

33 W. J. Mc Cormack, *Sheridan Le Fanu and Victorian Ireland* (Oxford, 1980), p. 9.

34 For a life of Whately, see William John Fitzpatrick, *Memoirs of Richard Whately* (London, 1864), 2 vols.

35 Joseph Holloway, in his otherwise civilized, intelligent layman's diary of the Abbey Theatre, speaks of Synge's 'warped, cynical bent of mind', and sees him as an 'evil genius' whose work is a 'nasty dungheap' (*Joseph Holloway's Abbey Theatre*, Carbondale, IL, 1967, p. 81).

36 Owen Dudley Edwards, 'Impressions of an Irish Sphinx', in Jerusha McCormack (ed.), *Wilde the Irishman* (New Haven, CT, and London, 1988), p. 50.

37 In *The Aran Islands* (Dublin, 1907) Synge keeps his epistemological distance from the islanders, feeling at once an outsider and curiously at home. The islanders, although at home, talk mainly of the outside world, of America and the war, and speak English to their children when they can. Synge has no unified perspective on them: if he sees them as tropical seabirds, he also notes that washing in sea water gives them rheumatism. He idealizes their freedom from crime and the 'medieval' beauty of their hand-made objects, but not their material conditions or cruelty to animals. The whole style of the book is understated, anti-heroic, focused on the trivia of daily life rather than on dramatic crises. Similarly, in his writings on Wicklow, Synge idealizes the vagrant as a natural aristocrat but is also keenly aware of class

distinctions in the countryside.

38 Susan Mitchell, *George Moore* (Dublin, 1916), p. 68. For a study of Mitchell, see Richard M. Kain, *Susan Mitchell* (Lewisburg, PA, 1972). Mitchell, the daughter of a Protestant banker from Shannon, speaks of Bernard Shaw as 'having his infallibilities', and fantasizes about the police being called into a theatre to break up a protest against a play which shows the Irish as virtuous and thus robs them of their reputation for unbridled ferocity. In her study of George Moore she wonders whether he had actually written his *Hail and Farewell* before coming to Ireland. See also Robin Skelton, 'Aids to Immortality: the Satirical Writings of Susan L. Mitchell', in Robin Skelton and Ann Saddlemyer (eds), *The World of W. B. Yeats* (Dublin, 1965).

39 See Raymond Williams, *Culture and Society 1780–1950* (Harmondsworth, 1958, reprinted 1963), pp. 178–80, 264.

40 Mc Cormack, *Sheridan Le Fanu and Victorian Ireland*, p. 7.

41 Samuel Ferguson, 'A Dialogue between the Head and Heart of an Irish Protestant', *Dublin University Magazine*, reprinted in Seamus Deane (ed.), *The Field Day Anthology of Irish Writing* (Derry, 1988), vol. 1, pp. 1178, 1183.

42 Mc Cormack, *Field Day Anthology*, vol. 1, p. 1176.

43 See the anonymous introduction to the journal in Walter E. Houghton (ed.), *Wellesley Index of Victorian Periodicals* (Toronto, 1987), p. 194.

44 *DUM*, 6 December 1835.

45 A rather similar case in point is Shelley's *Address to the Irish People* (1812), in which this revolutionary anarchist patronizes his Dublin audience by telling them to beware of drink and secret societies, practise moderation and develop a virtue and wisdom from which emancipation will automatically follow. He desires the restoration of Irish liberties 'so far as they are compatible with the English Constitution', insists that change has to be gradual and admonishes the Irish to foster a spirit of 'awe and caution'. He also roundly denounces the Catholic Church, for which he was hissed. Much of this might have been said by the luminaries of the *DUM*.

46 Michael Sadleir, p. 63.

47 See Barbara Hayley, 'Irish Periodicals from the Union to the *Nation*', *Anglo-Irish Studies*, no. 2 (1976).

48 See Charles Gavan Duffy, *Thomas Davis: Memoirs of an Irish Patriot 1840–1846* (London, 1890), p. 55.

49 See, for example, the precious, heavy-handedly 'witty' contributions of John Francis Waller, collected under the pseudonym Jonathan Freke Slingsby as *The Slingsby Papers* (Dublin, 1852).

50 See J. C. Beckett, *The Anglo-Irish Tradition* (London, 1976), for a general account of Anglo-Irish intellectual life. For further valuable scholarship

on the journal, see *The Long Room*, nos 14–15 (Trinity College Dublin, Autumn 1976 to Summer 1977).

51   Mortimer O'Sullivan, *Letter to Daniel O'Connell, Esq, by a Munster Farmer* (Dublin, 1824). See also his *Remains*, ed. J. C. Martin and M. O'Sullivan, 3 vols (Dublin, 1853), another study in panic-striken political reaction. In the third volume of this work, O'Sullivan defends the penal laws, claims that Catholic Emancipation has thwarted the whole process of the Reformation in Ireland, compares Irish agitators unfavourably to Indian Thuggees (who at least kill their victims quickly) and states that the Protestants of Ireland feel themselves abandoned. See also his *Guide to a Gentleman in His Search for a Religion* (Dublin, 1833), a dusty answer to Thomas Moore, and his *Case of the Protestants in Ireland* (London, 1836), which argues that the poverty of Roman Catholics is not enough to account for their perfidy.

52   Quoted in Wilfred Ward, *Aubrey de Vere* (London, 1904), p. 137.

53   Quoted in Peter Denman, *Samuel Ferguson: the Literary Achievement* (Gerrards Cross, 1990), p. 4. JohnWilson Croker had earlier registered his opinion that 'in politics, words are things' (*A Sketch of the State of Ireland Past and Present*, Dublin, 1808, p. 55). Croker remarks in this work that in Ireland 'the real danger is in those who cannot read, the true security in those who can' (p. 36). In this sense too, culture is an antidote to politics.

54   Lady Wilde, *Social Studies* (London, 1893), p. 13.

55   Ibid., p. 45.

56   Ibid., p. 111.

57   Ibid., p. 161.

58   Ibid., p. 172.

59   For a rare treatment of her writings, see Marjorie Howes, 'Tears and Blood: Lady Wilde and the Emergence of Irish Cultural Nationalism', in Tadhg Foley and Sean Ryder (eds), *Ideology and Ireland in the Nineteenth Century* (Dublin, 1998). See also Horace Wyndham, *Speranza: a Biography of Lady Wilde* (London, 1951), which records her desire to burn down Dublin Castle.

60   Lady Wilde, *Ancient Legends, Mystic Charms and Superstitions of Ireland* (London, 1887), vol. 1, p. 11.

61   *Driftwood from Scandanavia* (London, 1884), p. 225.

62   Lady Gregory (ed.), *Ideals in Ireland* (London, 1901), p. 11.

63   Gregory's nationalist conscience was first stirred outside Ireland, in Egypt, rather as she first met Yeats in London, not Dublin. Synge first encountered nationalist ideas in France, and Maud Gonne's first introduction to a distinctly unsavoury right-wing nationalist politics happened there too. But despite her experiences of Egyptian nationalism, Gregory remained unimpressed by Parnell and the Land League,

a discrepancy which her political comrade Wilfred Blunt was to remark on. In 1893 she published an anonymous pamphlet against Home Rule, but became a convert to the cause five years later. She worked zealously for the Gaelic League but viewed it as non-political, and defended Synge's *The Playboy of the Western World* while privately detesting it. A doughty worker among the destitute of London, she also spent much of her time indulging in genteel-nationalist talk at fashionable aristocratic dinner parties. Her *Memoirs* range from cricket to the Boer War, theosophy to whether galoshes are the thing to wear. She supported the Easter Rising much less ambiguously than Yeats, and had some sympathies for the Republican party in the civil war; but her plays are full of gullible stage-Irish and fondly indulged scamps. Adopting the proletarian Sean O'Casey in a somewhat *de haut en bas* manner, she remarked that his drama made her glad to have been born. See Ann Saddlemyer and Colin Smythe, *Lady Gregory: 50 Years After* (Gerrards Cross, 1987); Lady Gregory, *Our Irish Theatre* (London, 1914), *Journals 1916–30* (London, 1946) and Elizabeth Coxhead, *Lady Gregory: a Literary Life* (London, 1961).

64   An instance of this in the Revival is the extraordinary Edward Martyn, aristocrat, aesthete, ascetic, playwright, patron of the arts, misogynist and president of Sinn Fein. See D. Gwynn, *Edward Martyn and the Irish Revival* (London, 1930).

65   Emily Lawless, *Ireland* (London, 1912).

66   See 'Famine Roads and Memories', in *Traits and Confidences* (London, 1898).

67   The essay can be found in *Traits and Confidences*.

68   Aubrey de Vere, *English Misrule and Irish Misdeeds* (London, 1848), p. 36.

69   Ibid., p. 142.

70   Ibid., p. 206.

71   Aubrey de Vere, *Recollections* (London, 1897), chapter 16.

72   See Aubrey de Vere, *Essays, Chiefly Ethical and Literary* (London, 1889).

73   See *DUM*, vol. 4, no. 22 (October 1834).

74   See Lady Ferguson, *Sir Samuel Ferguson in the Ireland of his Day*, vol. 2, p. 187.

75   Tom Dunne, 'Haunted by History: Irish Romantic Writing 1800–50', in R. Porter and M. Teich (eds), *Romanticism in National Context* (Cambridge, 1988), p. 83.

76   Lecky's fellow Irish historian J. B. Bury, a Cambridge don and early Irish historical revisionist, insists on cutting the study of history loose from political rhetoric and establishing it instead on a soundly scientific basis. He considers Ranke's nationalism to cloud his historical judgement, and though not a Comtist or determinist, given his belief

in the historical role of chance and contingency, writes to some extent under the influence of Comte and Buckle. His attempt to rescue historiography from the rhetoricians in some ways parallels George Petrie's efforts to seize archaeology from the amateurs and politicos. See Bury's *Selected Essays* (Cambridge, 1930), especially 'The Science of History'.

77 W. E. H. Lecky, *Political and Historical Essays*, p. 11.
78 Ibid., p. 41.
79 Aubrey de Vere, *English Misrule and Irish Misdeeds*, p. 221.
80 The phrase is James Johnston Auchmuty's, in his *Lecky: a Biographical and Critical Essay* (Dublin, 1945), p. 2.
81 Donal McCartney, *W. E. H. Lecky: Historian and Politician 1838–1903* (Dublin, 1994), p. 45.
82 See Anne Wyatt, 'Froude, Lecky and the Humblest Irishman', *Irish Historical Studies*, vol. 19, no. 75 (March 1975), which points out the affinities as well as differences between the two historians.
83 Quoted in *A Memoir of the Right Hon. William Edward Hartpole Lecky, by His Wife* (London, 1909), p. 35.
84 John Elliot Cairnes, 'Mr. Comte and Political Economy', *Fortnightly Review* (May 1870).
85 W. E. H. Lecky, *History of the Rise and Influence of the Spirit of Rationalism in Europe* (London, 1865), vol. 1, p. xx.
86 W. E. H. Lecky, *History of European Morals from Augustus to Charlemagne* (London, 1869, reprinted New York, 1870), vol. 1, p. 60.
87 Ibid., p. 37.
88 Ibid., p. 113.
89 W. E. H. Lecky, *Political and Historical Essays*, p. 14.
90 See Alasdair MacIntyre, *A Short History of Ethics* (New York, 1966), *After Virtue* (London, 1981) and *Whose Justice? Which Rationality?* (London, 1988).
91 W. E. H. Lecky, *Political and Historical Essays*, p. 131. It is hard to know whether Lecky intends this image to be ironic.
92 See J. G. A. Pocock, *Virtue, Commerce, and History* (Cambridge, 1985).
93 W. E. H. Lecky, *History of the Rise and Influence of the Spirit of Rationalism in Europe*, vol. 2, p. 17.
94 Ibid., p. 93.
95 Ibid., p. 132.
96 Ibid., p. 33.
97 W. E. H. Lecky, *History of Ireland in the Eighteenth Century*, 5 vols (London, 1892–6). The work was extracted from Leckey's monumental *History of England*, 8 vols (London, 1878–90).
98 W. E. H. Lecky, *Political and Historical Essays*, pp. 87–8.
99 Ibid., p. 88.

100 W. E. H. Lecky, *Leaders of Public Opinion in Ireland* (London, 1861, reprinted NewYork, 1889), p. 126.

101 Ibid., p. viii.

102 'Anglo-Irish' here, as with Ferguson and de Vere, denotes a political position rather than an ethnic origin.

103 Standish O'Grady, *Toryism and Tory Democracy* (Dublin, 1886), p. 213.

104 'Irish Conservatism and Its Outlooks', in Standish O'Grady, *Selected Essays and Passages* (Dublin, 1918), p. 166.

105 Standish O'Grady, *The Crisis in Ireland* (Dublin, 1882), p. 50.

106 *Fortnightly Review*, no. 67 (February 1897).

Chapter 3 Savants and Society

1 W. E. H. Lecky, *History of European Morals from Augustus to Charlemagne* (London, 1869, reprinted New York, 1870), vol. 2, p. 167.

2 David Riesman, 'The Great Irish Clinicians of the 19th Century', *Johns Hopkins Hospital Bulletin*, vol. 24, no. 270 (August 1913), p. 2.

3 Davis Coakley, *The Irish School of Medicine* (Dublin, 1988), p. 141. See also his *Irish Masters of Medicine* (Dublin, 1992). For the disarray of Dublin medical studies before the advent of these men, see R. B. McDowell and D. A. Webb, *Trinity College Dublin, 1592–1952: an Academic History* (Cambridge, 1982), pp. 41–4, 87–9.

4 T. G. Wilson, *Victorian Doctor: Being the Life of Sir William Wilde* (London, 1942), p. 28.

5 Graves was the son of Richard Graves, who held Chairs in Divinity, Law and Greek at Trinity.

6 John Cheyne was a greatly distinguished Scottish physician at the Meath hospital, while Dominic Corigan wrote an important treatise on the aortic valve. As the Great Famine was taking hold, he warned the nation of the causal relation between famine and fever, at a time when this connection was not universally accepted. If the people are not supplied with food, he cautioned, 'pestilence' will surely follow. See his *On Famine and Fever as Cause and Effect in Ireland* (Dublin, 1846). Like many of his intellectual colleagues, Corrigan also wrote well on the question of university education.

7 Quoted in ibid., p. 79.

8 Ibid., pp. 80–1.

9 Ibid., p. 81.

10 William Stokes, *William Stokes: His Life and Work* (London, 1898), p. 21.

11 Whitley Stokes, *Projects for Re-establishing the Internal Peace and Tranquillity of Ireland* (Dublin, 1799), p. 44.

12 Ibid., p. 44.

13   Ibid., p. 47.

14   See his *A Reply to Mr Paine's 'The Age of Reason'* (Dublin, 1795), which addresses Paine's theism but not his politics, and musters some rather feeble arguments against it.

15   Whitley Stokes, *Observations on the Population and Resources of Ireland* (Dublin, 1821), p. 10.

16   Stokes emphasized how hard doctors had laboured during the Famine, and demanded higher pay for them. See his *Address Delivered in the Theatre of the Meath Hospital* (Dublin, 1847).

17   Stokes, *William Stokes: His Life and Work*, p. 87.

18   Thomas Carlyle, *My Irish Journey in 1849* (London, 1882), p. 41. The curmudgeonly tone of this work springs no doubt from the fact that Ireland represents everything that Carlyle's secularized Calvinism finds most abhorrent: chaos, untruth, shiftlessness, indolence, papist superstition, lower-class rebellion. The country is a veritable compendium of all the worst nightmares of one who believes in fact, truth, work, order, serfdom, strenuousness.

19   Lady Ferguson, *Sir Samuel Ferguson in the Ireland of His Day* (Edinburgh and London, 1896), vol. 1, p. 69.

20   See William Stokes, *Medical Education: an Address* (Dublin, 1861).

21   See William Stokes, *A Discourse Delivered at the Opening of the School of Physics in Ireland* (Dublin, 1864), p. 5. See also his *Introductory Address to the Royal College of Surgeons* (Dublin, 1855). An anonymous pamphlet of the time, *University Education in Ireland* (Dublin, 1861), argues that medical students who are deprived of humanistic education are 'separated by professional prejudices and interests from the other citizens of the commonwealth in which they live, and capable of forming only a partial and one-sided view of any topic outside the narrow limits of their caste' (p. 45).

22   This humanistic vista is recorded in Heney W. Ackland, *William Stokes: a Sketch* (London, 1882).

23   William Stokes, *State Medicine* (Dublin, 1872), p. 4.

24   Ibid., pp. 35–6.

25   See Vivian Mercier, *Modern Irish Literature* (Oxford, 1994), p. 29.

26   Whitley Stokes, *The Anglo-Indian Codes* (Oxford, 1888–9), vol. 1, pp. ix–x.

27   Quoted in Lady Ferguson, *Sir Samuel Ferguson in the Ireland of His Day*, vol. 2, p. 85.

28   Terence de Vere White, *The Parents of Oscar Wilde* (London, 1967), p. 72.

29   See Davis Coakley, *Oscar Wilde: the Importance of Being Irish* (Dublin, 1994), p. 19.

30   William Wilde, *Austria: Its Literature, Science, and Medical Institutions*

(Dublin, 1843).

31 William Wilde, *Narrative of a Voyage to Madeira, Teneriffe, and along the Shores of the Mediterranean* (Dublin, 1844), p. 222.

32 William Wilde, *On the Physical, Moral, and Social Condition of the Deaf and Dumb* (London, 1854), p. 5. The rather primitive nature of the medicine of the day is also illustrated by William Stokes's panacea for dysentry and diarrhoea during the Famine: a concoction of whiskey and laudanum diluted in two gallons of water, to which was added two pounds of logwood in chips (see Cormac Ó Gráda, *Black '47 and Beyond*, Princeton, NJ, 1999, p. 96). Ó Gráda comments that professional medicine, which did not at the time understand the mechanisms of infection, served little purpose during the Famine, and was sometimes worse than useless (p. 95).

33 William Wilde, *The Closing Years of Dean Swift's Life* (Dublin, 1849), p. 4.

34 William Wilde, *Ireland, Past and Present: the Land and Its People* (Dublin, 1864). p. 40.

35 Ibid., p. 50. Wilde speaks of himself in this volume as an Englishman.

36 William Wilde, *Lough Corib, Its Shores and Islands* (Dublin, 1872), p. 4.

37 For some of Sigerson's medical writings, see his *Collected Pamphlets* (Dublin, 1866–1904).

38 George Sigerson, *Modern Ireland, by an Ulsterman* (London, 1868), p. 384.

39 George Sigerson, *The Last Independent Parliament of Ireland* (Dublin, 1918), p. 10.

40 George Sigerson, *Bards of the Gael and Gall* (London, 1897), p. 41.

41 Ibid., p. 76.

42 Quoted in Daid Attis, 'The Social Context of W. R. Hamilton's Prediction of Conical Refraction', in Peter J. Bowler and Nicholas Whyte (eds), *Science and Society in Ireland* (Belfast, 1997), p. 24.

43 One might see Edmund Burke's political ideology as a remarkably dextrous attempt to back both cases at once. Social institutions have an ultimately divine sanction, but must adapt themselves pragmatically to evolving human circumstances.

44 Robert Perceval Graves, *Life of Sir William Rowan Hamilton*, 3 vols (Dublin, 1882), vol. 1, p. 267.

45 For Irish astronomical science, see Nicholas Whyte, 'Lords of Ether and of Light: the Irish Astronomical Tradition of the Nineteenth Century', *Irish Review*, nos 17/18 (1995). See also Patrick Moore, *The Astronomy of Birr Castle* (London, 1971).

46 See Terence de Vere White, *The Parents of Oscar Wilde*, p. 134.

47 I am grateful to my colleague Dr John Ockendon of St Catherine's College, Oxford, for discussing Hamilton's mathematical interests with me.

48 See Graves, *Life of Sir William Rowan Hamilton*, vol. 2, pp. 330–3.

49 Quoted in Lady Ferguson, *Sir Samuel Ferguson in the Ireland of His Day*, vol. 1, p. 70.

50 See Terence de Vere White, *The Parents of Oscar Wilde*, p. 128.

51 Quoted by James Bennett, 'Science and Social Policy in Ireland in the Mid-nineteenth Century', in Bowler and Whyte, p. 44.

52 Roy Johnston, 'Science and Technology in Irish National Culture', *The Crane Bag*, vol. 7, no. 2 (1983).

53 W. P. Ryan, *The Pope's Green Island* (London, 1912), p. 230.

54 See G. T. Wrixton, 'Irish Science and Technology: the Changing Role of the Universities', *Irish Review*, nos 17/18 (Winter 1995).

55 For those uncertain of the meaning of this term, it signifies spring-tailed land insects.

56 See A. S. Eve and C. H. Creasey, *The Life and Work of John Tyndall* (London, 1945). See also John Tyndall, *Fragments of Science* (London, 1879), 2 vols.

57 James Bennett, 'Science and Social Policy in Ireland in the Mid-nineteenth Century', in Bowler and Whyte, p. 40.

58 Wrixton, p. 119.

59 See Liam O'Dowd, 'Intellectuals in 20th Century Ireland: the Case of George Russell (AE)', in Richard Kearney (ed.), *The Crane Bag*, vol. 9, no. 1 (Dublin, 1985), p. 11.

60 See Gordon L. Herries Davies, 'Irish Thought in Science', in Richard Kearney (ed.), *The Irish Mind* (Dublin, 1985). One of the first Irishmen to spot the potential market for scientific popularization was the clergyman Dionysius Lardner, who produced no fewer than 133 such works and lectured on everything from John Locke to the steam engine. The playwright Dion Boucicault, probably his illegitimate son, inherited his sense of a mass audience.

61 Quoted in D. O. Raghallaigh, *Sir Robert Kane* (Cork, 1942), p. 7. It is doubtful that those in Dublin Castle concerned with agrarian secret societies shared this view.

62 Quoted in T. S. Wheeler, 'Sir Robert Kane: His Life and Work', *Studies*, vol. 33, no. 129 (March 1944), Part 1, p. 167.

63 The piece is reprinted as 'The Resources of Ireland' in C. P. Meehan (ed.), *Literary and Historical Essays by Thomas Davis* (Dublin, n.d.).

64 Sir Robert Kane, *Inaugural Address, Queen's College, Cork* (Dublin, 1849), p. 6. Henry Hennessy, brother-in-law of William K. Sullivan, argues in his *On Freedom of Education* (Dublin, 1859) the liberal Catholic view that each religious party must be free to organize its education in its own way. An anonymous pamphlet, *University Education in Ireland* (Dublin, 1861), claims that the Queen's colleges will not flourish without a strong basis in secondary education, and holds that the

grant for their establishment should be turned over to the secondary system in order to 'make the schools of Ireland worthy to rank with the Grammar Schools of England' (p. 29). Hennessy, who was largely self-taught, was professor of mathematics at the Royal College of Science.

65 See Isaac Butt, *Intellectual Progress*, p. 9.

66 Ibid., p. 9.

67 Trinity College had gradually modernized itself since the turn of the century, so that by mid-century about 10 per cent of its student body was Catholic. But they could not be scholars, and Fellowships were still restricted to those in Anglican orders.

68 Ibid., p. 12.

69 Ibid., p. 15.

70 See T. S. Wheeler, 'Sir Robert Kane: His Life and Work', Part 2, p. 325.

71 See Richard Kirwan, *Elements of Mineralogy* (London, 1784), the first systematic treatise on the subject in English.

72 See P. J. McLaughlin, 'Richard Kirwan: 1733–1812', *Studies*, vol. 28, no. 109 (March 1939). See also John Wilson Foster (ed.), *Nature in Ireland* (Dublin, 1997), pp. 124–5. Kirwan's brother was reputedly killed in a duel in a London coffee house.

73 See Richard Kirwan, *An Essay on Human Happiness* (Dublin, 1810).

74 See also his own monograph, *The Manufacture of Beet-root Sugar in Ireland* (Dublin, 1851).

75 William K. Sullivan, *University Education in Ireland* (Dublin, 1866), p. 5. The final phrase is no doubt an allusion to Protestant support for the 'godless' Queen's colleges.

76 Tristram Kennedy and William K. Sullivan, *Industrial Training Institutions of Belgium* (Dublin, 1855), p. 8.

77 See T. S. Wheeler, 'Life of William K. Sullivan', *Studies*, vol. 34, no. 133 (March 1945), p. 25.

78 See *Atlantis: a Register of Literature and Science by Members of the Catholic University of Ireland* (London, 1858), 4 vols.

79 See *Atlantis*, vol. 2 (1859), p. 127.

80 See William K. Sullivan, 'From the Treaty of Limerick to the Establishment of Legislative Independence', in R. Barry O'Brien (ed.), *Two Centuries of Irish History 1691–1870* (London, 1907). George Sigerson took up the narrative from there to the Union.

Chapter 4 The Dismal Science

1 William Thompson, *An Inquiry into the Principles of the Distribution of Wealth Most Conducive to Human Happiness* (London, 1824), p. xxix.

2 Ibid., p. xxvii.

3   Ibid., p. xx.

4   A late inheritor of this lineage is Thomas Kettle, professor of national economics at the National University in Dublin, whose humane, civilized writings on economics refuse to dissociate the science from questions of general human welfare. See in particular 'The Economics of Nationalism', in *The Day's Burden* (Dublin, 1910), in which Kettle contrasts the evident absurdity of a national mathematics or biology with the reasonableness of recognizing that, when it comes to economics, every country has 'its own flora and fauna'. The self-assured England which gave birth to classical political economy, he remarks, was as unconscious of its nationality as a healthy man is of his digestion, and therefore spuriously universalized what were in truth highly specific conditions.

5   William Dillon, *The Dismal Science* (Dublin, 1882), p. 13.

6   Butt also played a leading role in the amnesty campaign for Irish political prisoners. See his pamphlet *Ireland's Appeal for Amnesty* (London, 1870). He also wrote on the university question, advocating the addition of a Catholic college to Dublin University. See *The Problem of Irish Education* (London, 1875).

7   Thomas Carlyle, *My Irish Journey in 1849*, p. 54.

8   Christoper Morash comments that political economy for John Mitchel was 'purely a signifier of colonial hegemony', its scientific status 'subjugated to its instrumental role in the present exercise of power' (*Writing the Irish Famine*, Oxford, 1995, p. 66).

9   Isaac Butt, *A Voice for Ireland: the Famine in the Land* (Dublin, 1847), p. 11.

10 *Land Tenure in Ireland: a Plea for the Celtic Race* (Dublin, 1866), p. 42.

11 These are repeated claims in Butt's *The Irish People and the Irish Land* (Dublin, 1867), a response to criticism of his earlier work by Lord Dufferin and Lord Rosse.

12 Philip Bull, *Land, Politics and Nationalism* (Dublin, 1996), p. 67.

13 *Land Tenure in Ireland*, pp. 43–4.

14 Ibid., p. 101.

15 *The Irish People and the Irish Land*, p. 24.

16 W. E. H. Lecky, *Political and Historical Essays*, p. 93.

17 A link was provided, however, by his sales: his *Easy Lessons on Money Matters* was by far the best-selling work on economics in the nineteenth century. See Thomas A. Boylan and Timothy P. Foley, *Political Economy and Colonial Ireland* (London and New York, 1992), p. 4.

18 See Richard Whately, *Introductory Lectures on Political Economy* (London, 1831). The versatile Whately also wrote on rhetoric, to which he adopts an interestingly Wittgensteinian or anti-essentialist approach. 'Rhetoric' denotes no single object; there are legitimately different

uses of the term; and there is no 'real' object here independent of our conceptions about it, just as there is no 'natural' order of words. See *Elements of Rhetoric* (Oxford, 1828). Whately was described by one liberal-minded Irish commentator as 'a goodly specimen of the foreign vermin we have allowed to crawl over us'. Quoted in T. A. Boylan and T. P. Foley, 'J. E. Cairnes, J. S. Mill and Ireland', in A. E. Murphy (ed.), *Economists and the Irish Economy* (Blackrock, 1984), p. 114.

19 He later held a chair of political economy at University College, London, as well as chairs of political economy and jurisprudence at University College, Galway. Cairnes was born in County Louth in 1823, studied at Trinity College, and died in London in 1875. For commentaries on his work, see R. D. Collison Black, *Economic Thought and the Irish Question 1817–1870* (Cambridge, 1960), and Thomas A. Boylan and Timothy P. Foley, *Political Economy and Colonial Ireland* (London and New York, 1992).

20 See John Elliot Cairnes, 'Mr Comte and Political Economy', *Fortnightly Review* (May 1870).

21 See 'Political Economy as a Branch of General Education', in *Political Essays*.

22 John Elliot Cairnes, *Political Essays* (London, 1873), p. 7.

23 '*Ceteris paribus*' for philosophy of science means that scientific hypotheses can be said to be true only on certain conditions, with other things assumed to be equal. One assumes, for example, that neither the mouse nor the experimenter was intoxicated at the time. One of Cairnes's pupils recalled him as always stressing that 'circumstances alter cases', and 'never to forget one's *ceteris paribus*' (quoted in R. D. Collison Black, p. 55n).

24 See John Elliot Cairnes, *The Character and Logical Method of Political Economy* (London, 1857).

25 John Elliot Cairnes, 'Mr Spencer and the Study of Sociology', *Fortnightly Review* (1 February 1875), p. 205.

26 Ibid., p. 9.

27 John Elliot Cairnes, 'Mr Spencer on Social Evolution', in *Political Essays*.

28 A similar impatience with abstract universals marks the work of Lecky, who writes that 'there are no errors more common or more fatal than the political pedantry which estimates institutions exclusively by their abstract merits, without any regard to the special circumstances, wishes, or characteristics of the nations for which they are intended' (*Leaders of Public Opinion in Ireland*, New York, 1889, p. viii).

29 Quoted in R. D. Collison Black, p. 55. Black's classic study, despite the promise of its title, deals more with practical and historical matters than with the economic theories of Irish economists.

30 See John Elliot Cairnes, Review of Froude's *The English in Ireland*, *Fortnightly Review* (1 August 1874).

31 John Elliot Cairnes, *Essays in Political Economy, Theoretical and Applied* (London, 1873), p. 244.

32 Ibid., p. 249.

33 Cairnes praises the French political economist Bastiat's defence of free trade against the 'grim visage' of socialism, but criticizes him also as an ideologist. Bastiat wants to justify the workings of the economy, not just explain them, whereas Cairnes regards himself as having no 'foregone conclusions'. Bastiat, in short, confounds fact and value in a non-Kantian way, a distinction which Cairnes himself is keen to uphold. See 'Mr Comte and Political Economy', pp. 307ff. See also his pamphlet *England's Neutrality in the American Contest* (London, 1864), a drily legal disquisition by Cairnes's other persona as a professor of jurisprudence.

34 See John Elliot Cairnes, *The Slave Power* (London, 1863). The book is dedicated to the greatest of English liberals of the day, John Stuart Mill.

35 John Elliot Cairnes, *The Revolution in America* (Dublin, n.d.), p. 14.

36 Ibid., p. 44.

37 Ibid., p. 39.

38 W. E. H. Lecky, *Political and Historical Essays* (London, 1908), p. 11.

39 See 'Colonisation and Colonial Goverment', in John Elliot Cairnes, *Political Essays* (London, 1873).

40 *Essays in Political Economy*, p. 264.

41 Quoted in Boylan and Foley, p. 111.

42 Ibid., p. 262.

43 Ibid., p. 263.

44 John Elliot Cairnes, *Leading Principles of Political Economy Newly Expounded* (London, 1874), p. 321.

45 John Elliot Cairnes, *University Education in Ireland* (Dublin, 1866), p. 30.

46 Reprinted in *Political Essays*, p. 37.

47 Ibid., p. 39.

48 Cairnes supplied the material on Ireland for the sixth edition of Mill's *Principles of Political Economy*, and the two men shared a liberal line on the Fenians. See George O'Brien, 'J. S. Mill and J. E. Cairnes', *Economica*, vol. 10, no. 40 (November 1943). See also E. D. Steele, 'John Stuart Mill and the Irish Question', *Historical Journal*, vol. 13, no. 2 (1970).

49 The reviewer Robert Ellis Thompson, an American radical despite his reference to David Ricardo as a 'Jewish stockbroker', accuses Cairnes of political compromise, reluctant as he is to acknowledge that English political economy needs to be overturned in its very foundations. See

his review of Cairnes's *Some Leading Principles of Political Economy* in the *Penn Monthly* (September 1874). Conversely, an anonymous commentator on the same work claims that it is impossible to abolish the Irish landlords, a race which has always existed and always will (*A Few Remarks on Professor Cairnes's Recent Contribution to Political Economy*, London, 1875).

50 R. D. Collison Black, p. 54.
51 See R. D. Collison Black, 'Trinity College, Dublin, and the Theory of Value, 1832–1863', *Economica* (12 August 1943), p. 431. See also Laurence S. Moss, 'Mountiford Longfield's Supply-and-demand Theory of Price and Its Place in the Development of Brecon Theory', *History of Political Economy*, vol. 6, no. 4 (Winter, 1974).
52 Mountiford Longfield, *Four Lectures on Poor Laws* (Dublin, 1834), p. 35. See also Antoin E. Murphy, 'Mountiford Longfield's Appointment to the Chair of Political Economy in Trinity College Dublin, 1832', in Antoin E. Murphy (ed.), *Economists and the Irish Economy*, and R. D. Collison Black (ed.), *The Economic Writings of Mountiford Longfield* (New York, 1971).
53 See R. D. Collison Black, 'The Irish Dissenters and Nineteenth-century Political Economy', in Antoin E. Murphy (ed.), *Economists and the Irish Economy*, p. 133.
54 Thomas Edward Cliffe Leslie, *Essays in Political Economy* (Dublin and London, 1888), p. 21. See also G. Moore's essay on Cliffe Leslie in the *Journal of the History of Economic Thought*, no. 17 (Spring 1995).
55 Cliffe Leslie, *Essays in Political Economy*, p. 178–9.
56 Ibid., p. 240.
57 James Hardiman writes of the 'chaste, elegant, and pure' Irish love songs included in his *Irish Minstrelsy* that 'to the fascinating influence of these songs has been attributed many of the early marriages, and much of the "superabundant" population of our country. This, no doubt, will be deemed a new discovery in the science of political economy, and as such, is respectfully offered to the grave consideration of the Malthuses and Hortons of our day' (*Irish Minstrelsy*, Dublin, 1831, p. 202).
58 T. E. Cliffe Leslie, *Land Systems and Industrial Economy* (London, 1870), p. 90.
59 Ibid., p. 7.
60 Ibid., pp. 115, 128.
61 Thomas Carlyle, *My Irish Journey of 1849*, p. 53.
62 In an obituary notice of 1907, quoted in C. L. Falkiner, *Memoirs of John Kells Ingram* (Dublin, 1907).
63 Another was Henry Dix Hutton, who wrote on Irish agrarian issues but also on Comte. See his *The Religion of Humanity* (London, 1870),

Comte, The Man and the Founder (London, 1891) and *Comte's Life and Work* (London, 1892). Hutton corresponded with Comte, and some of the letters are to be found in Frederick Harrison (ed.), *Auguste Comte: Letters to Henry Dix Dutton* (London, 1901).

64 John Kells Ingram, *Practical Morals: a Treatise* (London, 1904), p. 9.

65 John Kells Ingram, *History of Political Economy* (Edinburgh, 1888), p. 9.

66 John Kells Ingram, *A History of Slavery and Serfdom* (London, 1895). Ingram regards slavery as morally speaking a 'monstrous aberration', but also sees it as having been materially essential, since without it productive industry would not have been developed. It was thus acceptable in its day, even if it has now become wrong since antiquated by progress. He does, however, allow that the transition from slavery to serfdom constituted a 'great and beneficent revolution'.

67 Ibid., p. 34.

68 Ibid., p. 153.

69 Ingram refers to Cairnes as 'English'.

70 Though the Postivist embracing of an empiricist epistemology threatens to undermine the school's scientific ambitions. Ingram writes elsewhere that we can know nothing with absolute certainty; in Humean fashion, we can know the world only as it affects us, and he is equally Humean in his view of causality. See his *Human Nature and Morals According to Auguste Comte* (London, 1901), chapter 1.

71 *Practical Morals: a Treatise*, p. 43.

72 John Kells Ingram, *Practical Morals: a Treatise*, p. 17. Ingram speaks in this work of the 'philosophy' of the child as 'fetishistic' (p. 21), meaning that children enjoy playing with toys.

73 John Kells Ingram, *Considerations on the State of Ireland* (Dublin, 1864), p. 17.

74 John Kells Ingram, *Human Nature and Morals According to Auguste Comte* (London, 1901), p. 43.

75 Ibid., p. 45.

Chapter 5 Young Irelanders and Others

1 See Patricia Boyce, *John O'Donovan 1806–1861, a Biography* (Kilkenny, 1987), and *Life and Labours of John O'Donovan* (Dublin, 1862), an anonymous pamphlet reprinted from the *DUM* which supplies the main facts of his career. There is a note on O'Donovan in Charles A. Read, *The Cabinet of Irish Literature* (London, 1880), vol. 3.

2 'There is a mad priest somewhere about Drumgoolan, that I am very anxious to see, as he is a native, and profound scholar. Dr. Crolly has silenced him for his love of wine, and I am told that he wanders about without any settled habitation' (John O'Donovan, *Letters Containing*

Information Related to the History and Antiquities of the County of Down in 1834 (Dublin, 1909), p. 50. The *Sligo Letters* (Dublin, 1926), *Meath Letters* (Dublin, 1927) and a number of the accounts of other counties are equally erudite and amusing.

3   Ibid., p. 51.

4   Vivian Mercier, *Modern Irish Literature* (Oxford, 1994), p. 13.

5   For Petrie's musicological activities, see Aloys Fleischmann, 'Petrie's Contrbution to Irish Music', *Proceedings of the Royal Irish Academy*, vol. 72, section C, no. 9 (Dublin, 1972). See also Harry White, *The Keeper's Recital* (Cork, 1998), pp. 63–5.

6   See Grace J. Calder, *George Petrie and the Ancient Music of Ireland* (Dublin, 1968), p. 16.

7   William Stokes, *Life and Labours of George Petrie* (London, 1868), p. 396.

8   David Greene, 'George Petrie and the Collecting of Irish Manuscripts', *Proceedings of the Royal Irish Academy*, vol. 72, section C, no. 7 (Dublin, 1972).

9   The phrase is Joep Leerssen's, in his *Imagination and Remembrance* (Cork, 1996), p. 104. Leerssen's meticulously researched study is by far the best account of the subject.

10   Quoted in Lady Ferguson, *Sir Samuel Ferguson in the Ireland of His Day*, p. 60.

11   Terence de Vere White, *The Parents of Oscar Wilde*, p. 178.

12   Quoted in Lady Ferguson, p. 63. Douglas Hyde's presidency of the Gaelic League somewhat later is perhaps the last great moment of this ascendancy of the intellectual gentry in Gaelic studies.

13   Ibid., p. 66.

14   Ibid., p. 61.

15   Stokes, *Life and Labours of George Petrie*, p. 98. The bookseller and antiquarian John O'Daly, editor of the acclaimed *Poets and Poetry of Munster* (Dublin, 1849), was patronized in a rather more positive sense of the word, receiving financial support from a benefactor of Celtic studies; but he also challenged the rather exclusive *milieu* of this world by founding the Ossianic Society as a cheaper, more popular alternative to the Irish Archaeological Society. Vivian Mercier describes the Ossianic Socierty as 'the most democratic body yet organised for Irish studies' (*Modern Irish Literature*, p. 22).

16   See David Lloyd, *Nationalism and Minor Literature: James Clarence Mangan and the Emergence of Irish Cultural Nationalism* (Berkeley, CA, 1987). For Mangan's reflections on identity, see D. J. O'Donoghue, *Prose Writings of James Clarence Mangan* (Dublin, 1904), p. 285.

17   For this experimental, irreverent strain in Irish translation, see Michael Cronin, *Translating Ireland* (Cork, 1996).

18   D. J. O'Donoghue (ed.), *Poems of Mangan* (New York, 1859), p. xv.

19 Ibid., p. xliv.

20 For an instance of Mangan's feeble, laboured wit, see his 'Treatise on a Pair of Tongs', in D. J. O'Donoghue, *Prose Writings of James Clarence Mangan*.

21 James Fintan Lalor, *Collected Writings* (Washington, DC, 1997), p. 97.

22 Quoted in Richard Davis, *The Young Ireland Movement* (Dublin, 1987), p. 259. See also Charles Gavan Duffy, *Young Ireland: a Fragment of Irish History 1840–1850* (London, 1896) and *Thomas Davis: the Memoirs of an Irish Patriot 1840–46* (London, 1890). A recent study of Davis is John N. Molony, *A Soul Came into Ireland: Thomas Davis, 1814–1845* (Dublin, 1995).

23 See Richard Kearney, 'Between Politics and Literature: the Irish Cultural Journal', *The Crane Bag*, vol. 7, no. 2 (Dublin, 1983).

24 Arthur Griffith (ed.), *Meagher of the Sword* (Dublin, 1917), p. 35.

25 The Irish Brigade's reputation for valour is noted by Simon Winchester in his *The Professor and the Madman* (London, 1998), p. 56.

26 Quoted in James Fintan Lalor, *Collected Writings*, p. 123. A valuable contemporary account of Lalor is to be found in David N. Buckley, *James Fintan Lalor: Radical* (Cork, 1990).

27 James Fintan Lalor, *Collected Writings* , p. 4.

28 See Meagher's essays 'On the Union' and 'The O'Connellites', in *Meagher of the Sword*.

29 Lalor, *Collected Writings*, p. 102.

30 Ibid., p. 63.

31 Morash, p. 59.

32 For a life of Mitchel, see William Dillon, *Life of John Mitchel* (London, 1888), 2 vols.

33 John Mitchel, *United Irishman*, quoted in William Dillon, vol. 1, p. 211. The finest analysis of Mitchel's prose style is to be found in Christopher Morash, *Writing the Irish Famine* (Oxford, 1995), pp. 66–75.

34 See Arthur Griffith (ed.), *Meagher of the Sword*, p. 202.

35 Ibid., pp. 227–8.

36 John Mitchel, *The Last Conquest of Ireland (Perhaps)* (Dublin, 1861, reprinted Glasgow, n.d.), p. 33.

Index